ocm58452018

DISCARD

CAMPBELL COUNTY PUBLIC LIBRARY
RUSTBURG, VIRGINIA

MOVING PEOPLE, THINGS, AND IDEAS

A History of
Powered Ships

MOVING PEOPLE, THINGS, AND IDEAS

Other Books in the Series:

A History of Aircraft
A History of Sailing Ships
A History of Water Travel

MOVING PEOPLE, THINGS, AND IDEAS

A History of
Powered Ships

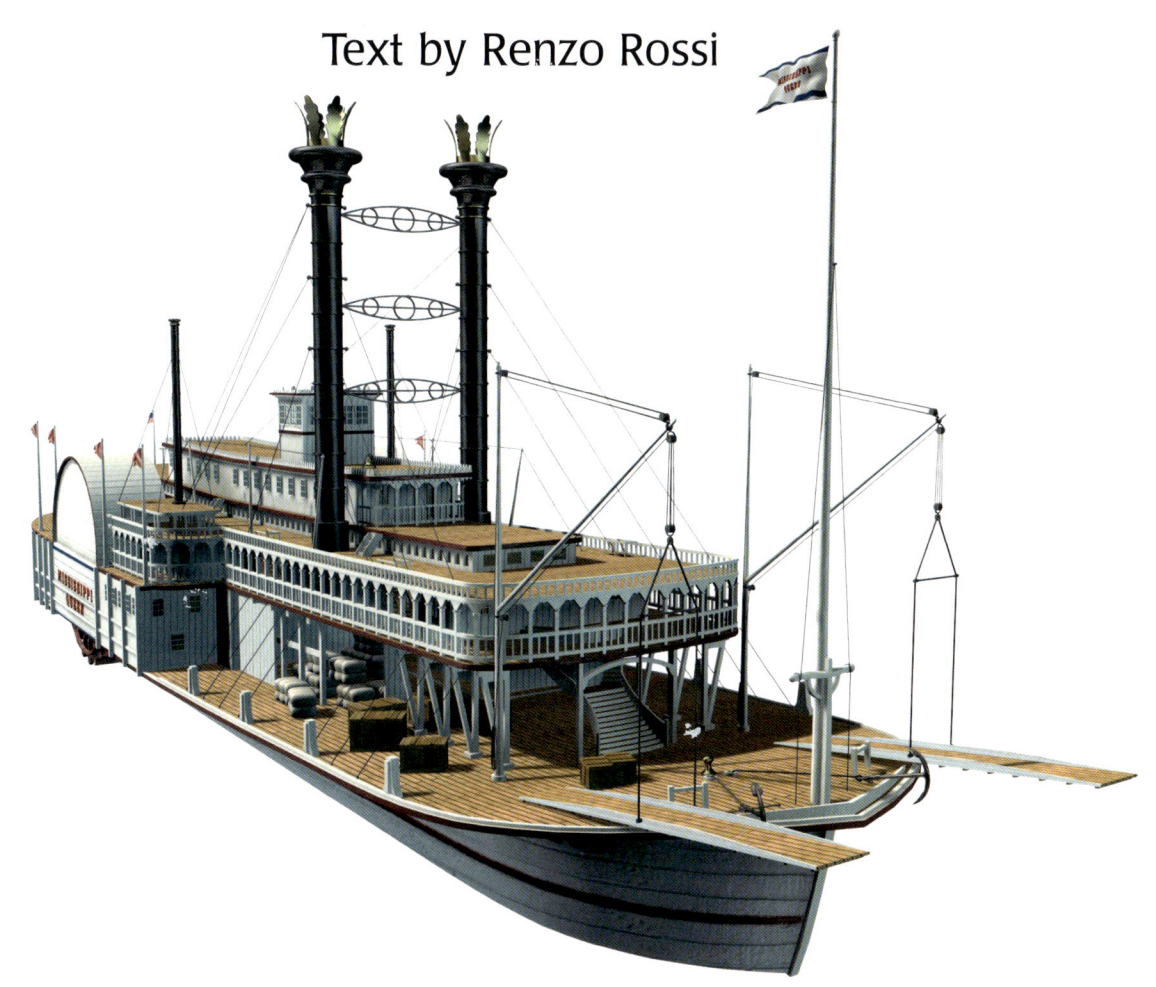

Text by Renzo Rossi

BLACKBIRCH PRESS
An imprint of Thomson Gale, a part of The Thomson Corporation

THOMSON
GALE

CAMPBELL COUNTY PUBLIC LIBRARY
RUSTBURG, VIRGINIA

Detroit • New York • San Francisco • San Diego • New Haven, Conn. • Waterville, Maine • London • Munich

THOMSON

GALE

Copyright © 2004 by Andrea Dué s.r.l., Florence, Italy

Published in 2005 in North America by Thomson Gale

All rights reserved

Conception and production: Andrea Dué s.r.l.
Text: Renzo Rossi
Translation: Erika Pauli
Illustrations: Alessandro Baldanzi, Alessandro Bartolozzi, Leonello Calvetti, Lorenzo Cecchi, Sauro Giampaia, Luigi Ieracitano, Roberto Simoni, Studio Stalio (Alessandro Cantucci)
Research, documentation, and layout: Luigi Ieracitano
Cutouts: Uliana Derniatina

Photo Credits: page 14, Corel Corporation; page 31, © Official U.S. Navy Photograph

Thomson and Star Logo are trademarks and Gale and Blackbirch Press are registered trademarks used herein under license.

For more information, contact
Blackbirch Press
27500 Drake Rd.
Farmington Hills, MI 48331-3535
Or you can visit our Internet site at http://www.gale.com

ALL RIGHTS RESERVED
No part of this work covered by the copyright hereon may be reproduced or used in any form or by any means—graphic, electronic, or mechanical, including photocopying, recording, taping, Web distribution or information storage retrieval systems—without the written permission of the publisher.

Every effort has been made to trace the owners of copyrighted material.

LIBRARY OF CONGRESS CATALOGING-IN-PUBLICATION DATA

Rossi, Renzo, 1940–
  A history of powered ships / by Renzo Rossi.
     p. cm. — (Moving people, things, and ideas)
  Includes bibliographical references and index.
  ISBN 1-4103-0660-7 (hardcover : alk. paper)
  1. Ships—Juvenile literature. 2. Motorboats—Juvenile literature. I. Title. II. Series.

VM150.R6277 2005
623.82'04—dc22

2005004570

Printed in the United States
10 9 8 7 6 5 4 3 2 1

Contents

BEYOND THE WIND	6
THE FIRST STEAMERS	8
IRON GIANTS	10
BATTLESHIPS	12
LUXURY LINERS	14
THE *TITANIC*	16
IN STEERAGE	18
FERRYBOATS, HYDROFOILS, AND HOVERCRAFTS	20
PORTS	22
SHIPS BUILT FOR SPECIAL TASKS	24
TANKERS	26
DEEP-SEA FISHING	28
SUBMARINES	30
UNUSUAL SHIPS	34
MODERN WARSHIPS	36
SUPPORTING WARSHIPS	38
AIRCRAFT CARRIERS	40
SIGNALS AT SEA	42
PLEASURE BOATS	44
GLOSSARY	46
FOR MORE INFORMATION	47
INDEX	48

Beyond the Wind

When people first began creating boats, they often relied on the wind as a source of power. But wind is unpredictable: Winds change direction, and sometimes there is no wind blowing. Over the centuries, people invented many new ways to make boats move. The Romans used paddle wheels driven by slaves. The paddles on these wheels revolved vertically, pushing backward against the water to move the boat forward. In ancient times, the Chinese used paddle wheels to power their flat-bottomed boats, called junks.

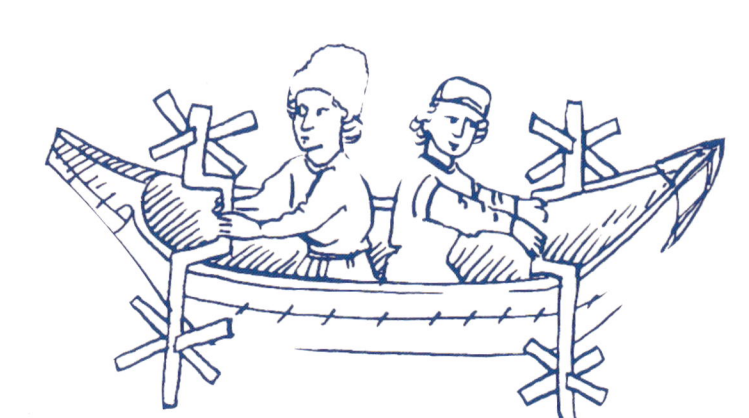

In the 15th century, the artist and inventor Leonardo da Vinci designed a boat with a large paddle wheel. This boat relied on strong sailors to turn a crank that caused the paddle wheel to turn. He thought his boat would move faster than one that was powered by men rowing with oars. But despite these new designs, muscle power was still required to move boats with paddle wheels. This remained a problem until the invention of the steamship. The steamship allowed boats to travel over longer distances, in any kind of weather, and with smaller crews.

Above: A drawing shows a model of a paddle-wheel boat based on Leonardo da Vinci's drawings. The boat was never built.

Above: A 15th-century drawing shows one inventor's idea for a device that could power a boat.

Below: A 16th-century drawing shows a junk powered by paddle wheels. The wheel was powered by slaves who turned it by walking on steps (right).

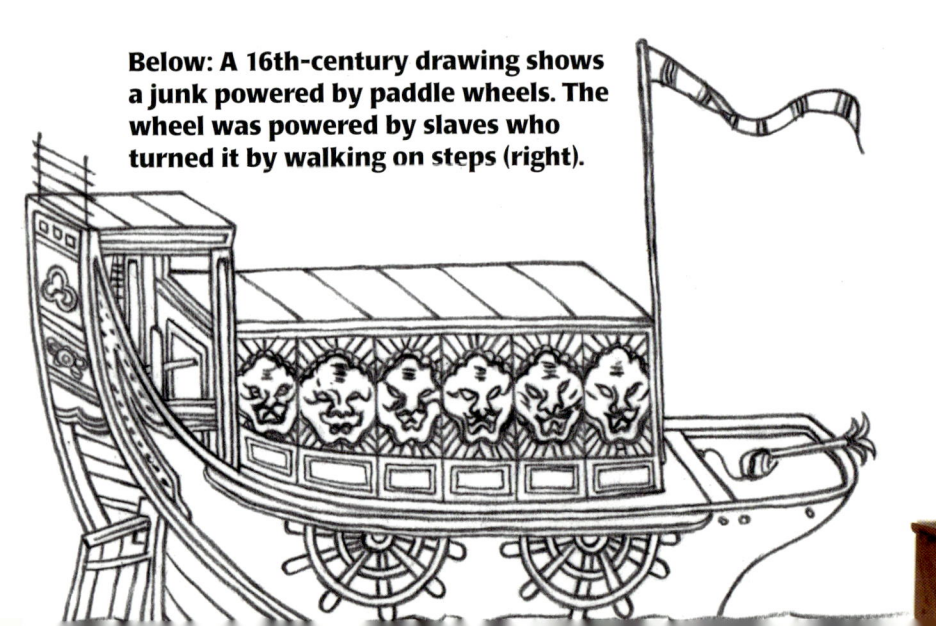

Chronology

Above: A drawing shows a French steamboat made in the late 1700s.

Above: A drawing shows the steamship *Arpad*, built in 1836.

Below, left: Englishman Joseph Braman patented his paddle wheel design in 1785. The pinwheel propeller, with its slanting vanes, could move ships forward or backward.

Below: A cutaway drawing shows a paddle-wheel ship from the mid-1800s. Steam from the boiler goes through a tube (a) into a cylinder (b). The steam pressure pushes a piston back and forth. The piston is connected by a shaft (c) to a crank (d) that changes the back-and-forth movement of the piston into a rotating movement that turns the paddle wheel (e).

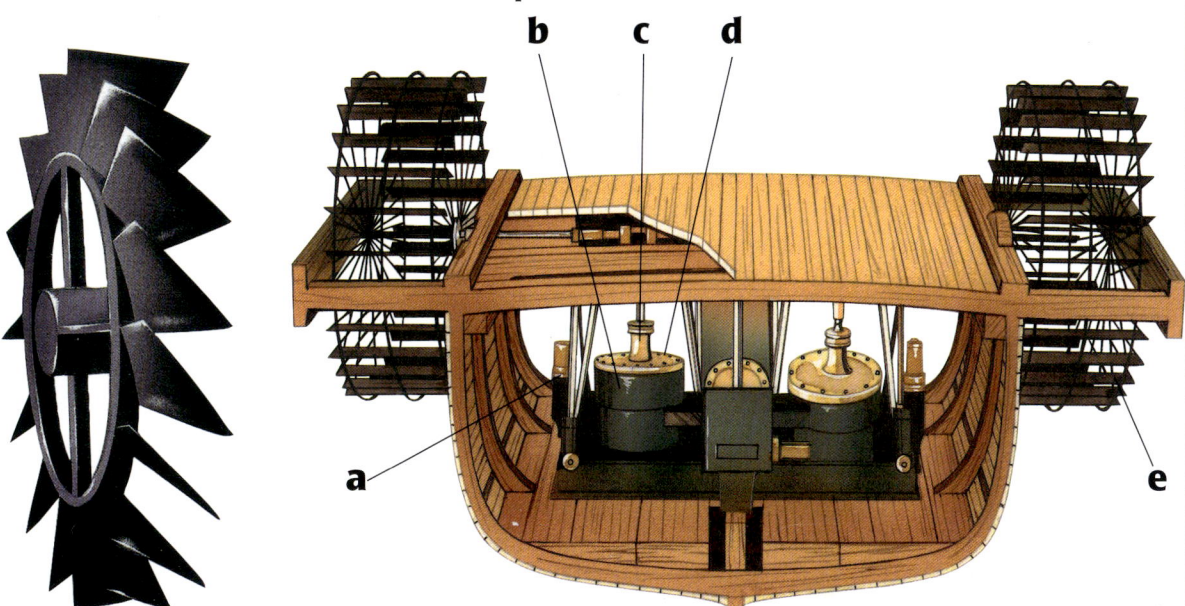

1685
French scientist and inventor Denis Papin designs the first cylinder-and-piston steam engine.

1736
Jonathan Hulls gets a patent for a machine that can carry ships into and out of the harbor. The tugboat used steam to move its paddle wheels.

1802
The *Charlotte Dundas*, a towing steamboat, is built. It tows two 70-ton barges nearly 20 miles (32.2km) in six hours.

7

The First Steamers

Robert Fulton, an American engineer and inventor, is credited with developing the first steam-powered ship. On August 17, 1807, Fulton's steamboat left New York City on the Hudson River, bound for Albany, New York. This was the beginning of steamboat service. The name of Fulton's first steamboat is usually given as the *Clermont*, but he called it the *North River Steamboat*. Soon after his steamboat's first appearance, ships like it began sailing on other rivers in the United States and in Europe.

In 1819, the steamship *Savannah* made the first successful voyage across the Atlantic Ocean. The *Savannah* traveled from Georgia to England in a journey that took 27 days and 11 hours. The ship had sails, and it did not use its engines very much because there was little room on board for the coal needed to fuel them.

Another steamship, the *Sirius*, crossed the Atlantic in 1838. The *Sirius* set out on April 4, with an additional 400 tons of coal. When the ship ran out of coal, the crew burned other supplies for fuel. Traveling at a speed of 6.7 knots it landed in New York after 18 days, welcomed by a great crowd.

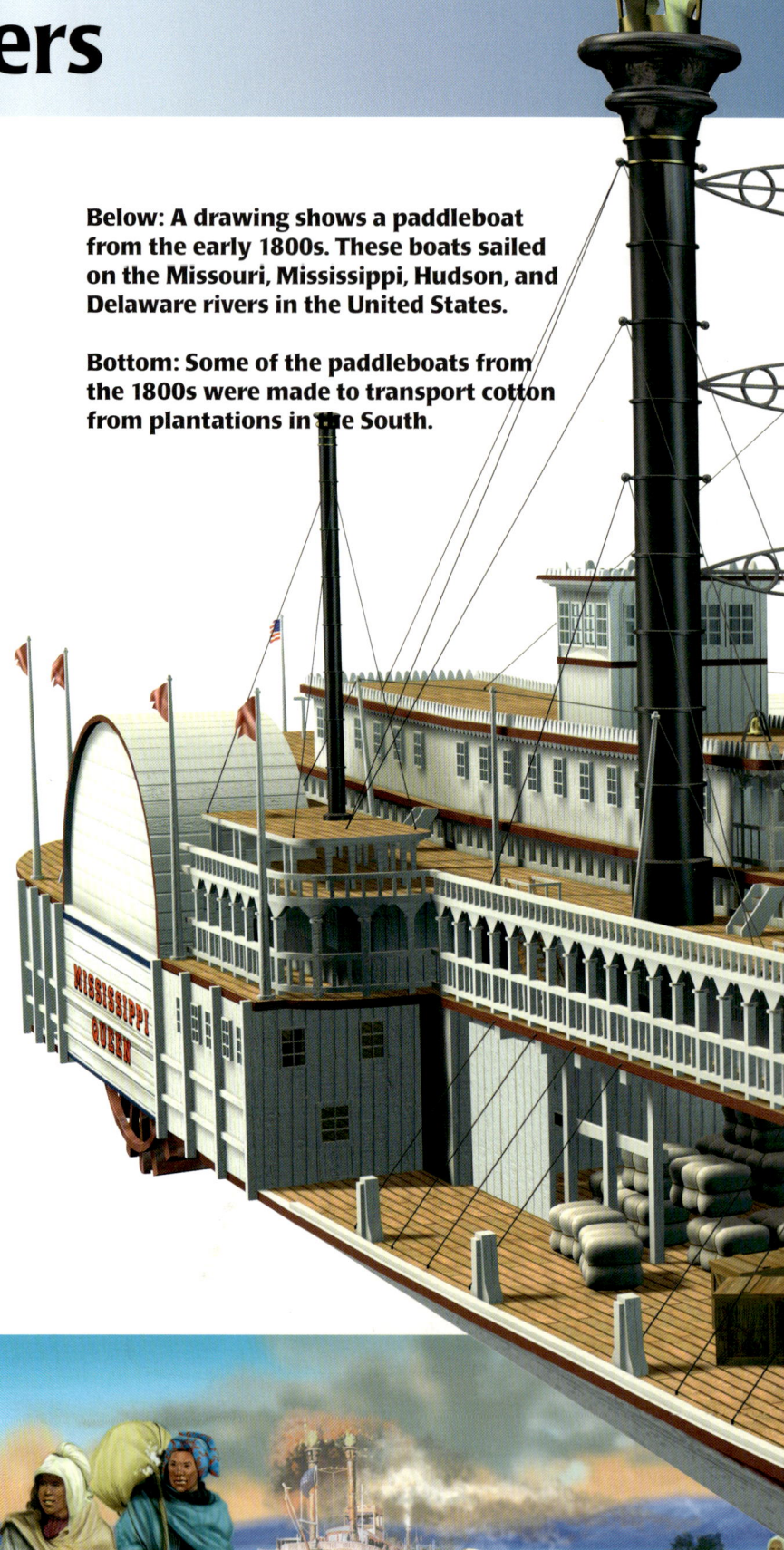

Below: A drawing shows a paddleboat from the early 1800s. These boats sailed on the Missouri, Mississippi, Hudson, and Delaware rivers in the United States.

Bottom: Some of the paddleboats from the 1800s were made to transport cotton from plantations in the South.

Chronology

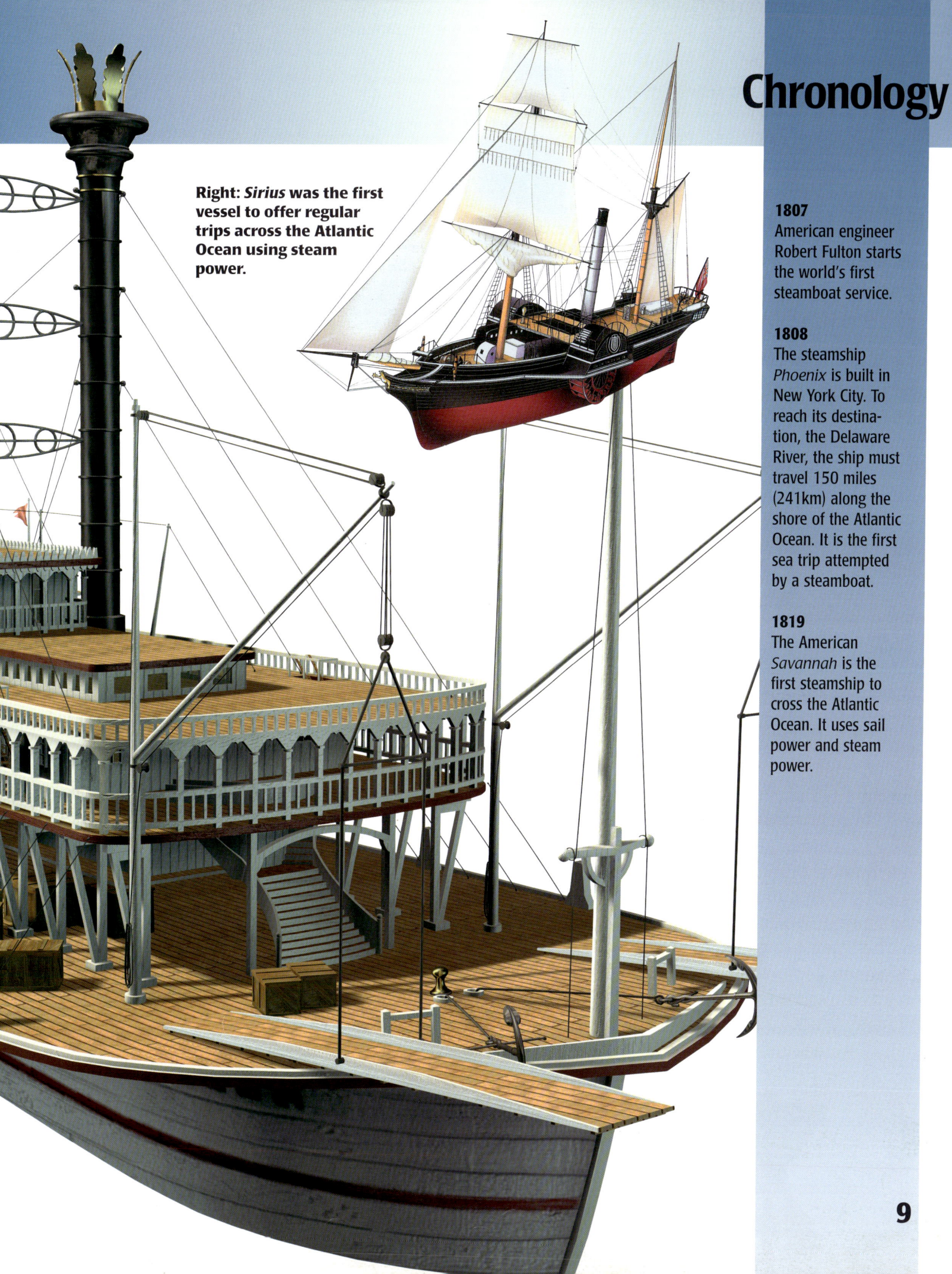

Right: *Sirius* **was the first vessel to offer regular trips across the Atlantic Ocean using steam power.**

1807
American engineer Robert Fulton starts the world's first steamboat service.

1808
The steamship *Phoenix* is built in New York City. To reach its destination, the Delaware River, the ship must travel 150 miles (241km) along the shore of the Atlantic Ocean. It is the first sea trip attempted by a steamboat.

1819
The American *Savannah* is the first steamship to cross the Atlantic Ocean. It uses sail power and steam power.

Iron Giants

In 1843, the English engineer Isambard Kingdom Brunel introduced the world to a new type of ship. He designed and built the steamship *Great Britain* to cross the Atlantic Ocean. The *Great Britain* was different from other steamships in several ways. First, it was built of iron rather than wood. And it used a new type of power. It was powered by propellers rather than by paddle wheels. Propellers worked better in rough seas and pushed ships forward faster. The *Great Britain* set a new standard for ocean travel, becoming the first propeller-powered ship to cross the Atlantic Ocean.

The success of the *Great Britain* led Brunel to try to create an even bigger ship. He gave it paddle wheels, propellers, and a giant hull of iron. At the time, people thought steamships could not carry enough coal to fuel very long ocean voyages. But the *Great Eastern* was able to carry 15,000 tons (13,608 metric tons) of coal. Construction of the ship began in 1854. The huge ship finally made its first journey across the Atlantic Ocean in 1860. The *Great Eastern* never became the famous passenger ship that Brunel had hoped it would be, but it did assist in laying telegraphic cables in oceans around the world for many years.

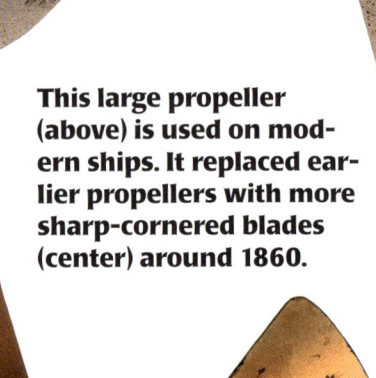

This large propeller (above) is used on modern ships. It replaced earlier propellers with more sharp-cornered blades (center) around 1860.

Chronology

Above: A drawing shows the steam engine that drove the paddle wheels of the *Great Eastern*. Each wheel was 56 feet (17m) tall and had 30 blades.

Below: The *Great Eastern* was 692 feet (211m) long and 85 feet (26m) wide at its widest point. The ship had six masts with 6,500 square yards (5,434.83 sq. m) of sails. It had five elegant salons and featured first-class cabins with hot and cold running water.

1800–1839
Steamship builders experiment with various types of propellers.

1822
The English-built SS *Aaron Manby* takes a test sail on the Thames River. It is the world's first iron steamship.

1845
The *Great Britain* becomes the first iron-hulled, propeller-driven steamship to cross the Atlantic Ocean.

1845
A British contest between two types of steamships pits the propeller-driven HMS *Rattler* against the paddle-driven HMS *Alecto*. The two ships are attached at the stern for a kind of tug of war. The *Rattler* wins.

1854
Construction of the *Great Eastern* begins in the ship-yards along the Thames River.

Battleships

Battleships were the most heavily armed and armored warships used. In 1860, France launched a new type of battleship. It was called *La Gloire (The Glory)*. The French wanted to build a ship with a hull made of iron, but settled on a wooden hull covered with iron plates. The French thought the ship would protect their crews from attack and help them dominate the seas. Instead, *La Gloire* inspired the British navy to begin building its own ironclad ship. The British HMS *Warrior* became the first warship with an iron hull to sail the world's oceans. It was the largest warship of its time.

Above: A cutaway drawing shows an interior view of the USS *Merrimack*. After a fire nearly destroyed the ship, it was rebuilt and clad with iron for use by the Confederate military during the Civil War. The ship was renamed the CSS *Virginia*.

Below: A drawing shows a midship section of the Union's *Monitor*, an ironclad ship that battled with the CSS *Virginia* during the Civil War.

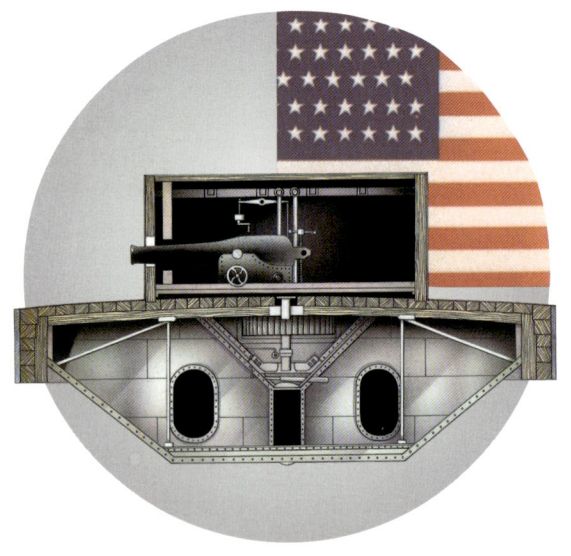

Below: On March 9, 1862, the ironclad warships the CSS *Virginia* and the Union's *Monitor* fought one another in a fierce sea battle.

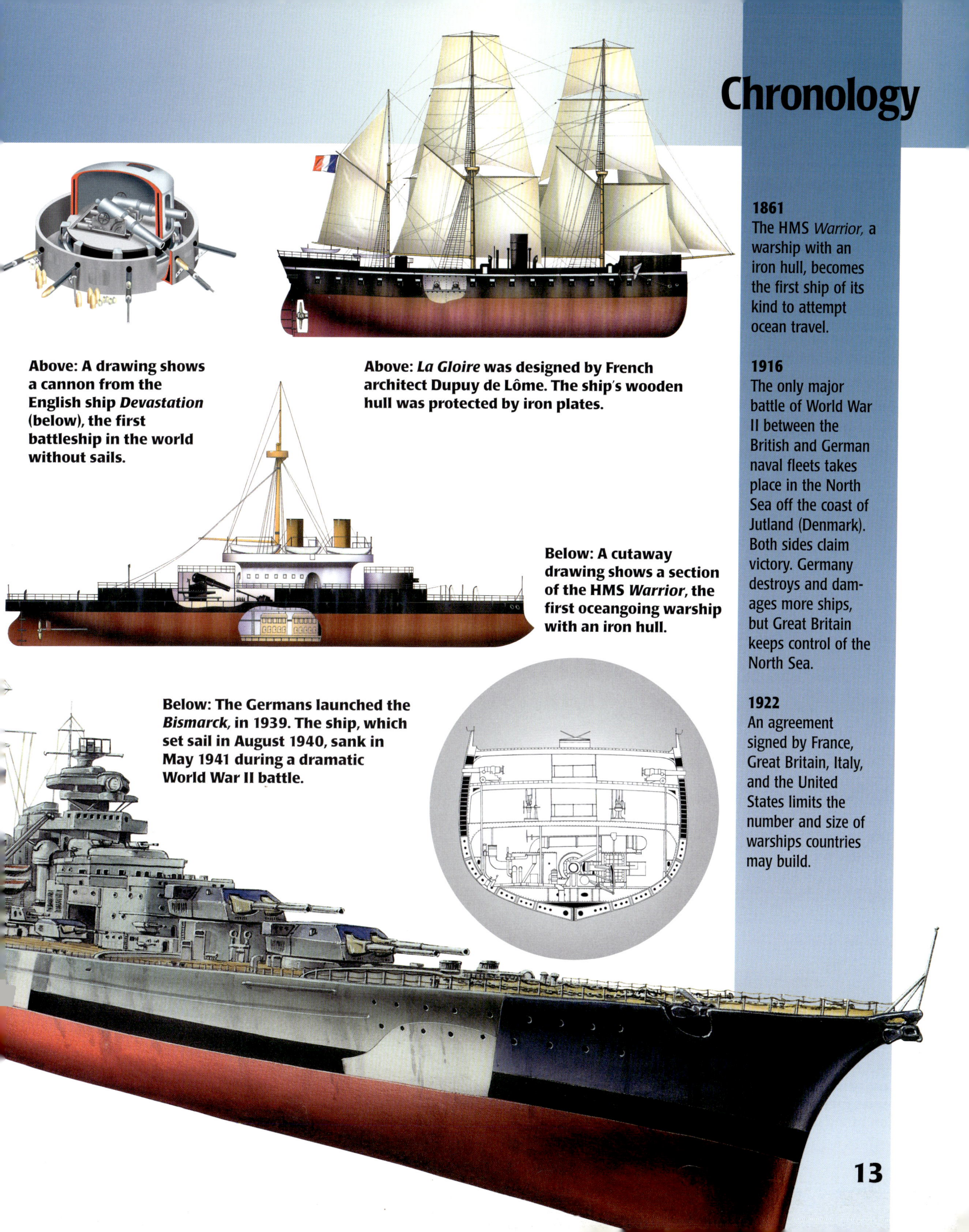

Chronology

Above: A drawing shows a cannon from the English ship *Devastation* (below), the first battleship in the world without sails.

Above: *La Gloire* was designed by French architect Dupuy de Lôme. The ship's wooden hull was protected by iron plates.

Below: A cutaway drawing shows a section of the HMS *Warrior*, the first oceangoing warship with an iron hull.

Below: The Germans launched the *Bismarck*, in 1939. The ship, which set sail in August 1940, sank in May 1941 during a dramatic World War II battle.

1861
The HMS *Warrior*, a warship with an iron hull, becomes the first ship of its kind to attempt ocean travel.

1916
The only major battle of World War II between the British and German naval fleets takes place in the North Sea off the coast of Jutland (Denmark). Both sides claim victory. Germany destroys and damages more ships, but Great Britain keeps control of the North Sea.

1922
An agreement signed by France, Great Britain, Italy, and the United States limits the number and size of warships countries may build.

13

Luxury Liners

The golden age of ocean liners began in the early 20th century and lasted until the 1960s. These large passenger ships were the main means of traveling from one continent to another for many years, until airplane travel became more common. Many ocean liners offered wealthy passengers luxurious places to sleep and eat. Passengers who did not have enough money to travel first-class were usually crowded into lower decks. Many immigrants traveled this way.

Right: The *Queen Mary*, launched in 1934, was one of the most luxurious ocean liners.

Above: The *Radisson Diamond* was launched in Finland in 1992. It is a Small-Waterplane-Area Twin-Hull (SWATH) ship. Because the ship has two hulls, passengers do not feel the sea's movement as much as they do on other ships.

14

Chronology

1907
The English ocean liner *Mauretania* takes to the sea. It is one of the largest and most luxurious ships of its day.

1932
The Italian ship *Rex* begins service. The *Rex* becomes the only Italian-built ship to win a trophy for the fastest crossing of the Atlantic Ocean, but its record is quickly surpassed by other ships.

1934
The English *Queen Mary*, one of the world's most luxurious ocean liners, makes its maiden voyage.

1935
The French ocean liner *Normandie*, the first ship to exceed 1,000 feet (304m) in length, makes its maiden voyage.

1940
Under a cover of gray paint, the *Queen Elizabeth* secretly sails from Great Britain to New York City. The ship serves in World War II until 1946, when it begins service as one of the world's most luxurious ocean liners.

Above: A replica of an American ocean liner from the 1950s became a child's toy.

The *Titanic*

The best-known ocean liner was the *Titanic*. It was the largest and most elegant ship of its day. It was a luxury hotel at sea. It had reading rooms, tearooms, a gym, a swimming pool, and ballrooms. On April 10, 1912, the *Titanic* set sail on its maiden voyage. It left Southampton, England, headed for New York City. The steamship had 2,227 passengers and crew aboard. At 11:40 P.M. on April 14, the ship struck an iceberg. Two hours and 40 minutes later, the ship sank. Because there were not enough lifeboats, 1,522 people were lost at sea, and only 705 people survived. A team of French and American researchers discovered the wreckage of the *Titanic* on September 1, 1985. The remains of the ship are more than 12,000 feet (3,658m) under the sea, about 350 miles (563 km) southeast of the Canadian province of Newfoundland.

Right: Newspapers around the world published front-page stories about the *Titanic* disaster.

Below: Although the White Star Line, which owned the *Titanic*, called the ship unsinkable, it sank on its very first transatlantic voyage. The ship was 885 feet (269.75m) long and had the most up-to-date technology. It had a double-bottomed hull and sixteen watertight compartments.

17

In Steerage

Ocean liners brought a wave of immigrants from Europe to America. The cheapest way to travel on the ships was on the lower decks of the ship, called steerage. The lower decks were called steerage because the steering mechanism of sailing ships had once been housed there. Huge steamships could hold thousands of passengers in the lower decks.

The people who owned ocean liners made a lot of money selling cheap tickets to immigrants. But the trip was a terrible experience for most immigrants. Steerage was crowded, dirty, and smelly. There were not enough toilet facilities. The journey across the ocean could last anywhere from ten days to a month, and many people became seasick. In 1911, the United States Immigration Commission wrote a report to President William H. Taft that described the conditions in steerage, saying, "It is a marvel that human flesh can endure it." Despite the poor conditions, immigrants took these journeys for the chance to begin a new life.

Above: Immigrants standing on the deck of an ocean liner headed for the United States during the early 20th century.

Below: A photograph shows three ocean liners on the dock in Southampton, on the English Channel, in the 1920s.

Left: An ocean liner's wind scoops bring fresh air to the interior of the ship.

Chronology

Above: A drawing shows the yacht *Elettra*. Guglielmo Marconi, the Nobel Prize–winning engineer from Italy, bought the ship in 1919 to serve as a laboratory for his experiments. Marconi invented the radio, the first practical wireless communications system. The radio became an important way for ships at sea to communicate with each other.

Right: Guglielmo Marconi used this transmission device (right) in one of his most famous demonstrations of instant wireless communication. In 1930, while aboard the *Elettra* harbored in Genoa, Italy, Marconi pressed a key on his transmitter that turned on thousands of colored lights in the town hall in Sydney, Australia.

1920
After its defeat in World War I, Germany is forced to give its ships to Great Britain and the United States.

1930
Third-class passengers on the Japanese ocean liner *Kamo Maru* travel between Japan and Australia and sleep on hammocks or mats called tatami.

1934
To make sure it is seen as a luxury liner, the *Queen Mary*, boards 1,600 first- and second-class passengers, but only 577 third-class passengers.

1940–1941
The British transform many ships, including the luxury ocean liners *Queen Elizabeth*, *Aquitania,* and *Mauretania,* into military transport ships.

19

Ferryboats, Hydrofoils, and Hovercrafts

Ferryboats allow people and freight to travel where land routes are interrupted by water. Some ferryboats are designed to hold cars and trucks. Passengers drive their vehicles across ramps onto the ferry. They travel with their cars or trucks across the water, and then drive off the ferry after it lands. In many coastal cities, ferryboats are an important part of the public transportation system.

A hydrofoil boat has wings mounted beneath its hull. The hydrofoil is a wing that flies in water. A hydrofoil boat has two ways to sail. It can sail like a regular boat, with its hull in the water. Or it can sail with its hull completely out of the water, with only the foils beneath the water. Because the hull of the boat does not drag through the water, hydrofoils sailing on their wings can travel very fast.

A hovercraft moves on a thin cushion of air. Some hovercraft travel over land, while others travel over water. Christopher Cockerell invented the modern hovercraft in 1952. The British inventor used a vacuum-cleaner motor and two cans in experiments that showed how a vehicle could ride a cushion of air. Hovercrafts can travel faster than many ships or land vehicles, but they need very smooth surfaces.

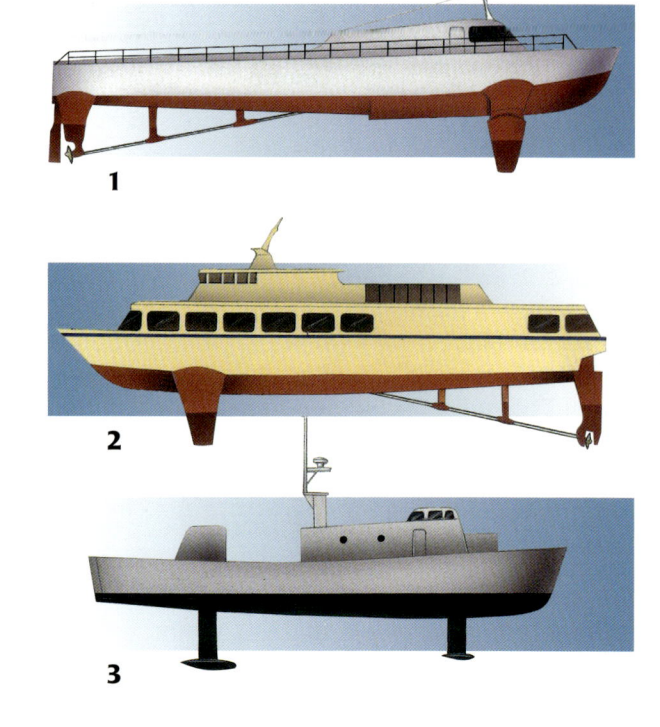

Above: Drawings show three kinds of hydrofoil designs.

Right: A modern ferryboat transports passengers, cars, trucks, locomotives, and railroad cars.

20

Chronology

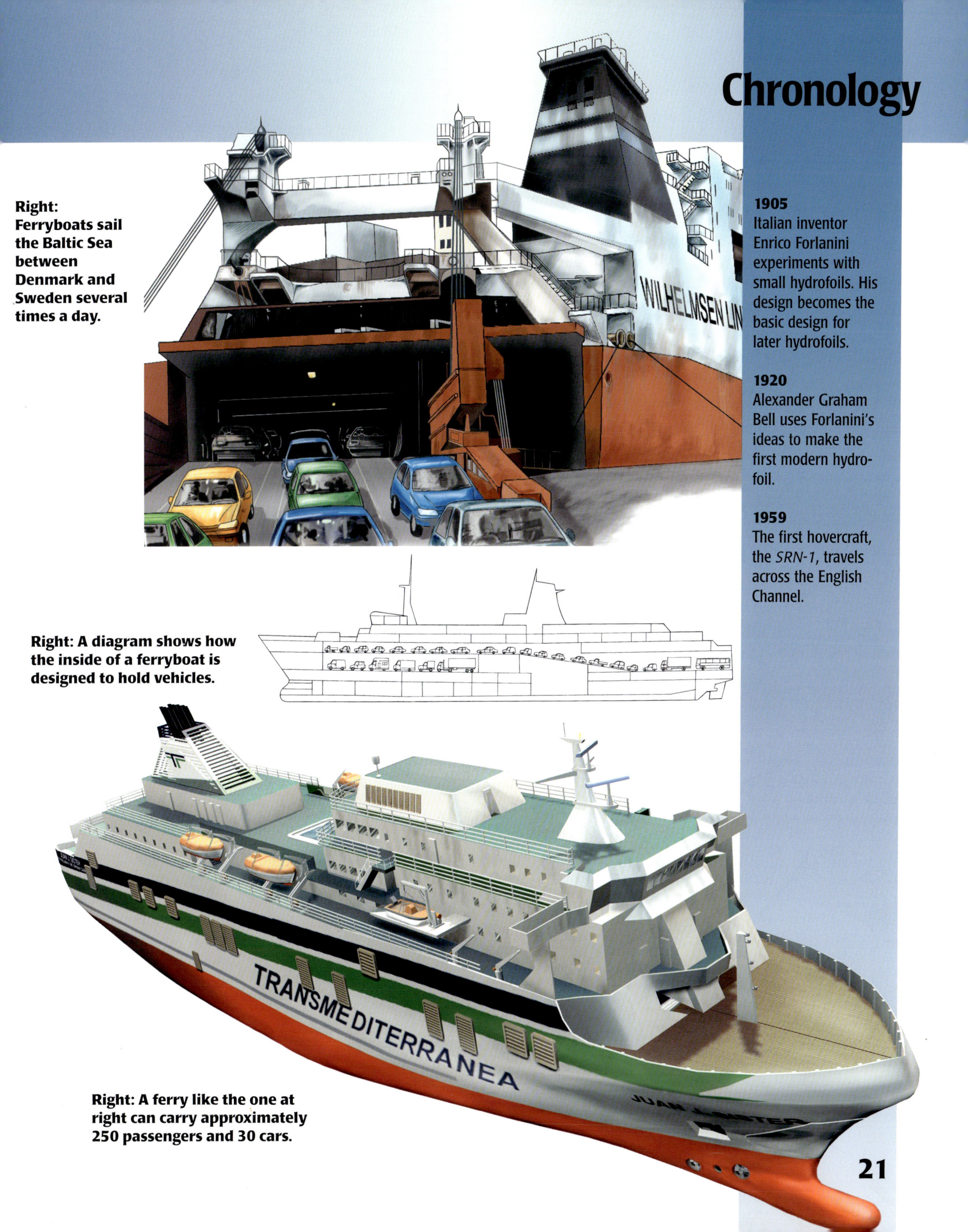

Right: Ferryboats sail the Baltic Sea between Denmark and Sweden several times a day.

1905
Italian inventor Enrico Forlanini experiments with small hydrofoils. His design becomes the basic design for later hydrofoils.

1920
Alexander Graham Bell uses Forlanini's ideas to make the first modern hydrofoil.

1959
The first hovercraft, the *SRN-1*, travels across the English Channel.

Right: A diagram shows how the inside of a ferryboat is designed to hold vehicles.

Right: A ferry like the one at right can carry approximately 250 passengers and 30 cars.

21

Ports

Ports are places at the edge of oceans, rivers, and lakes where ships can dock to load and unload cargo and passengers. Ports have many services that big ships need. They have special equipment that helps ships load and unload cargo. They have facilities for repair and maintenance of ships. Ports often have buildings in which cargo can be stored. They have special refrigerated storage facilities for fish and other goods that require it. Good ports need deep water to allow large ships to enter. They also need to offer ships protection from wind and waves. Some ports began in places where natural bays offered protection from rough, open water. Other ports were built by people.

Below, left: Drawings show a ship being launched from a dry dock, a place where ships can be taken out of the water for repair or maintenance.

Below, right: Longshoremen unload cargo in the 1920s. The job of longshoremen is to unload ships. The name is taken from the days when ships would pull into a port looking for men along the shore to unload cargo. Now, longshoremen use machinery to unload ships.

Opposite, top: A drawing shows a type of crane that is used in ports.

Below: A drawing shows the system a merchant ship uses to unload goods.

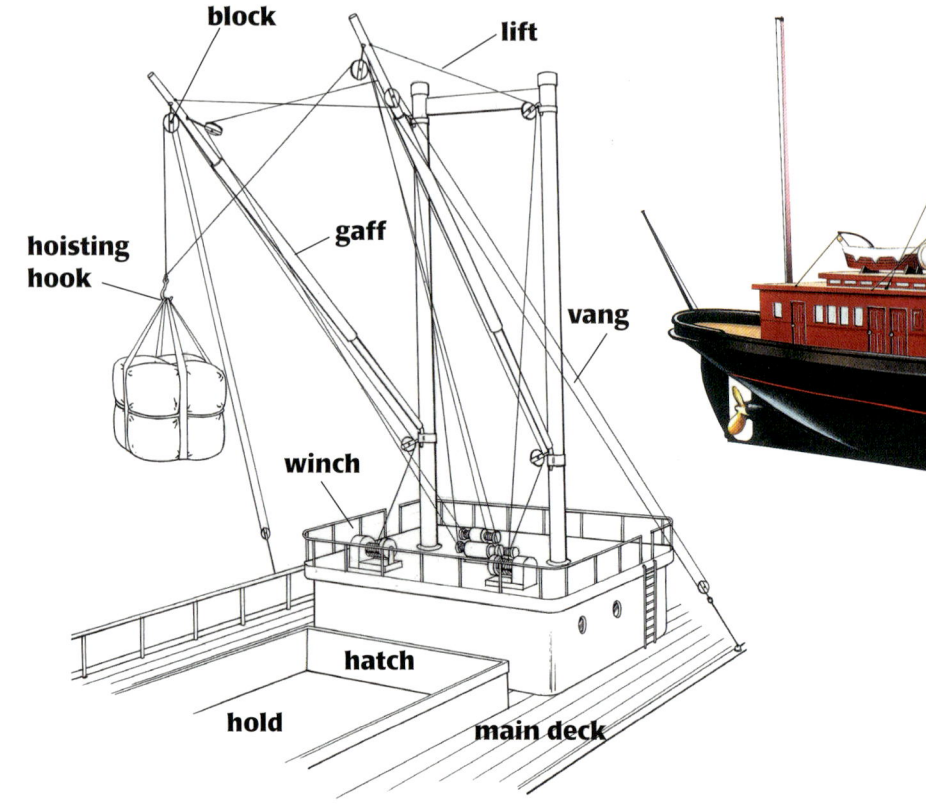

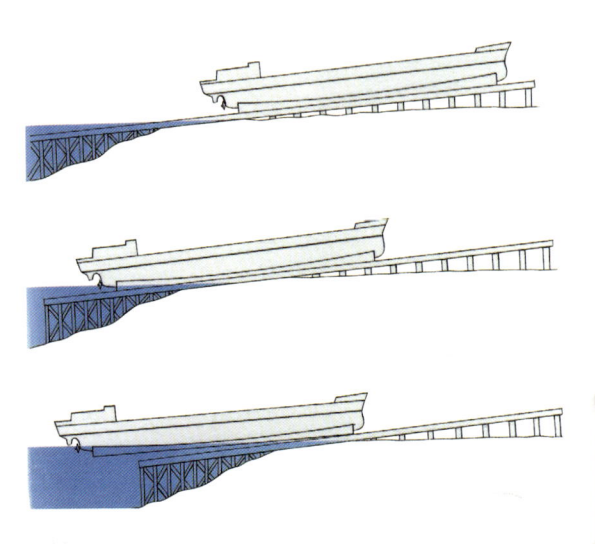

22

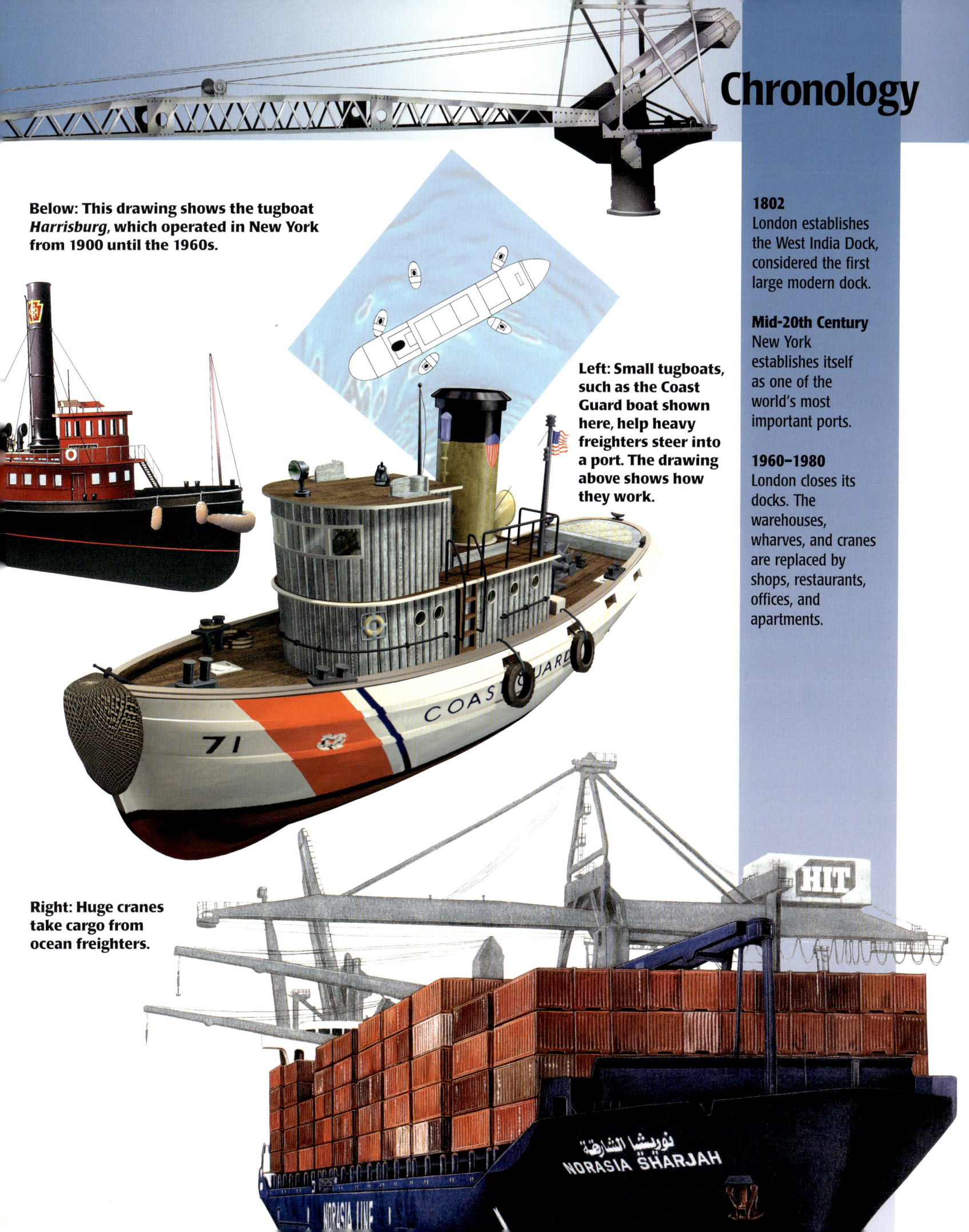

Chronology

Below: This drawing shows the tugboat *Harrisburg*, which operated in New York from 1900 until the 1960s.

Left: Small tugboats, such as the Coast Guard boat shown here, help heavy freighters steer into a port. The drawing above shows how they work.

Right: Huge cranes take cargo from ocean freighters.

1802
London establishes the West India Dock, considered the first large modern dock.

Mid-20th Century
New York establishes itself as one of the world's most important ports.

1960–1980
London closes its docks. The warehouses, wharves, and cranes are replaced by shops, restaurants, offices, and apartments.

Ships Built for Special Tasks

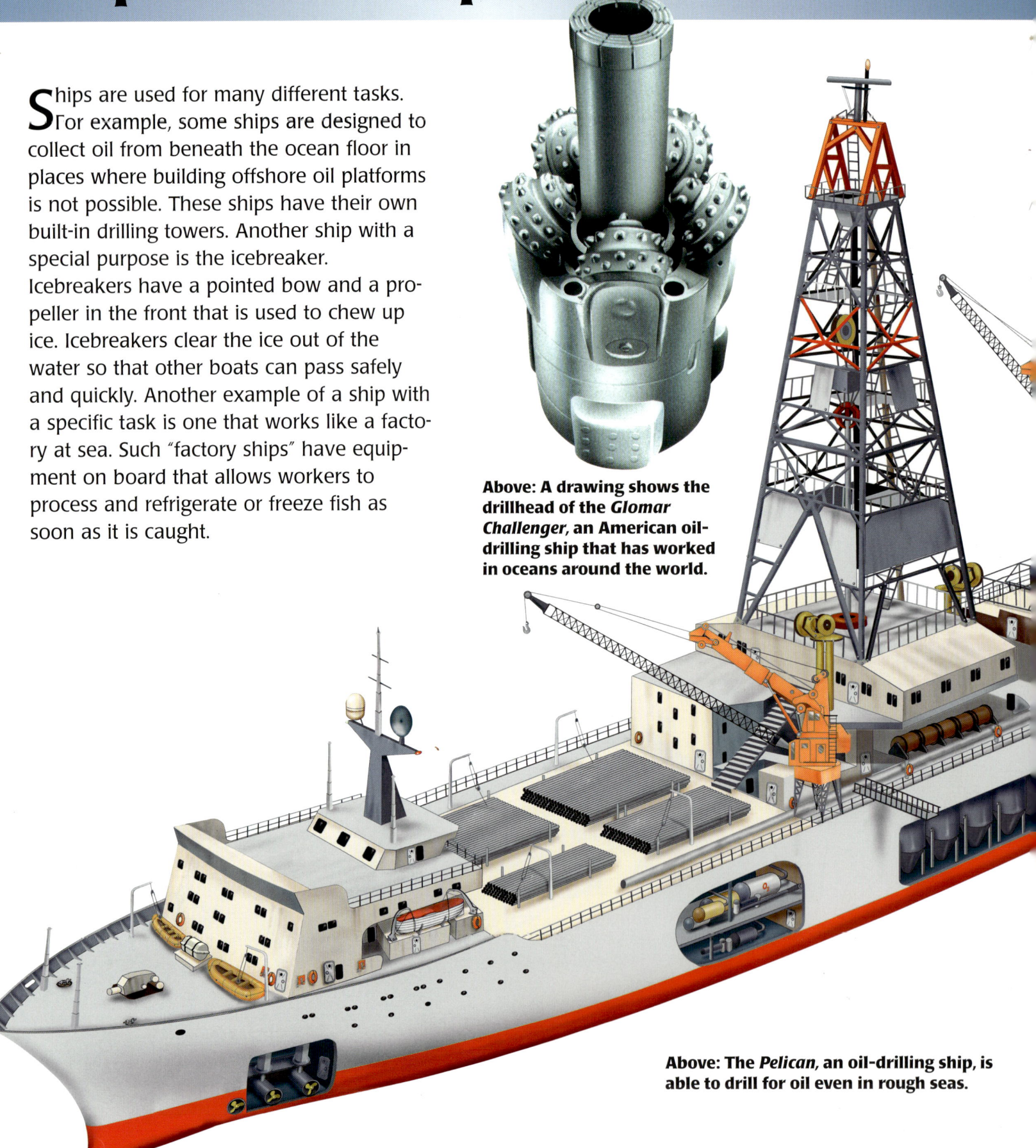

Ships are used for many different tasks. For example, some ships are designed to collect oil from beneath the ocean floor in places where building offshore oil platforms is not possible. These ships have their own built-in drilling towers. Another ship with a special purpose is the icebreaker. Icebreakers have a pointed bow and a propeller in the front that is used to chew up ice. Icebreakers clear the ice out of the water so that other boats can pass safely and quickly. Another example of a ship with a specific task is one that works like a factory at sea. Such "factory ships" have equipment on board that allows workers to process and refrigerate or freeze fish as soon as it is caught.

Above: A drawing shows the drillhead of the *Glomar Challenger*, an American oil-drilling ship that has worked in oceans around the world.

Above: The *Pelican*, an oil-drilling ship, is able to drill for oil even in rough seas.

Chronology

Above: Icebreakers are common sights in some regions of the United States, Canada, and the Scandinavian countries.

Right: A drawing shows the type of equipment used by a ship designed for ocean research.

- Satellite navigation
- Radar navigation
- Seismic detector
- Depth camera
- Sweeper
- Box sampler
- Buoy anchored with instruments for measuring the current, pressure, and temperature.

1871
The first efficient icebreaker is built in Amsterdam.

1910
The first ships for processing fish catches are used in the Pacific Ocean.

1947
Offshore drilling for oil begins in the Gulf of Mexico.

1968
The *Glomar Challenger*, an American oil-drilling ship, is launched.

1977
Offshore drilling begins in the North Sea.

Tankers

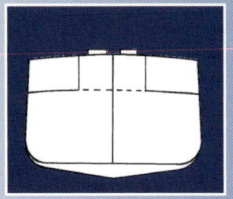

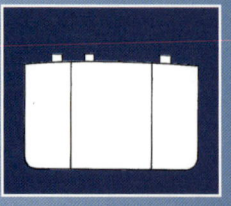

A tanker is a ship designed to carry liquid cargo. Tankers usually transport fuel oils. They carry crude oil from oil-producing regions of the world to other countries that need fuel. In 1886, the Germans built the world's first modern tanker, the *Glückauf,* which means "lucky" in German. Until the *Glückauf,* liquid cargo such as oil was shipped in barrels. The design of the *Glückauf* made it possible to put liquid fuel directly into the ship's hull. Today, some of the world's biggest ships are tankers. They are so large that they are sometimes called supertankers. In 1979, Japan built the *Jahre Viking*, the world's largest ship. The Japanese super-tanker can carry more than half a million tons (453,600 metric tons) of crude oil. It is said that if the Empire State Building were placed on its side, the *Jahre Viking* would be longer by 253 feet (77m).

The first modern tankers were single hulled. That is, they did not have a lining, which reduces the chance of leaking. People worried about leaking oil harming the environment have pushed to require tankers to be double hulled. Double-hulled tankers have a lining inside the outer hull. Those who enforce shipping standards around the world want all single-hulled tankers to be gone by 2015.

In 1989, when the oil tanker *Exxon Valdez* ran aground in Alaska, it was one of the most reported and studied environmental disasters in the world. The tanker spilled 11 million gallons (41.6 million l) of oil, enough to fill 125 Olympic-sized swimming pools. The spill fouled 1,300 miles (2,092km) of shoreline and killed birds, sea otters, harbor seals, bald eagles, salmon, herring, and killer whales. Though it was one of the largest spills to ever occur in the United States, there have been much larger oil spills in other parts of the world.

Above: A drawing shows an offshore oil platform.

26

Above: Drawings show how the compartments that hold fuel may be arranged in the hulls of tankers.

Above: A photograph shows a shipwrecked tanker leaking oil.

Below: A drawing shows a tanker with a double hull to prevent leaks and to reduce the amount of oil that is spilled if the ship wrecks.

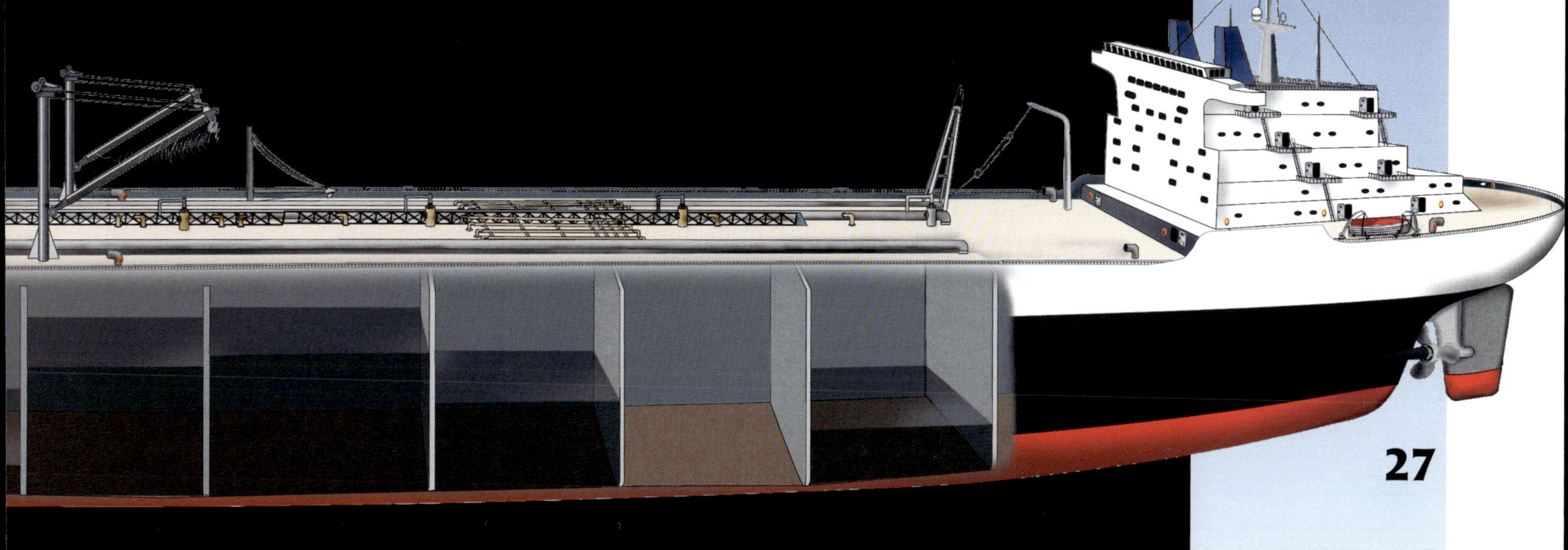

Chronology

1921
The *William Rockefeller*, one of the world's largest tankers, is launched. It can hold 22,600 tons (20,500 metric tons) of fuel.

1953
The *Tina Onassis* sets sail as the world's largest tanker. It can hold 45,750 tons (41,500 metric tons) of oil.

1965
England builds the *British Admiral*, a tanker that can hold 100,000 tons (90,718 metric tons) of oil.

1978
The Liberian ship *Amoco-Cadiz* wrecks off the coast of France and spills 23,000 tons (20,865 metric tons) of oil.

2002
The tanker *Prestige* splits in two off the coast of Spain and spills 70,000 tons (63,500 metric tons) of oil.

27

Deep-Sea Fishing

Commercial fishing boats today have modern equipment to help them find their prey. They find fish by using sonar. The letters in the word are taken from the phrase "**so**und **n**avigation **a**nd **r**anging." Sonar uses sound waves that are reflected by objects in the water to locate fish. Most of the fish are captured with trawling nets, long, cone-shaped nets that are dragged along the sea bottom by the boats. Sometimes the nets remain in mid-water. The best commercial fishing boats have computer equipment that places the nets at different depths to catch certain kinds of fish.

The devices fishing boats use to find and catch their prey work so well that some people worry about fish populations dying out. To protect some species of fish, governments sometimes ban the fishing of certain species or limit the number that can be caught. Sometimes governments try to get fishing boats to change the ways they fish. For example, the fishing techniques used to catch tuna have led to the deaths of dolphins. Tuna like to swim in schools beneath dolphins, which are often caught and killed in the huge tuna nets. The United States has a law that is meant to protect dolphins from being caught and killed this way.

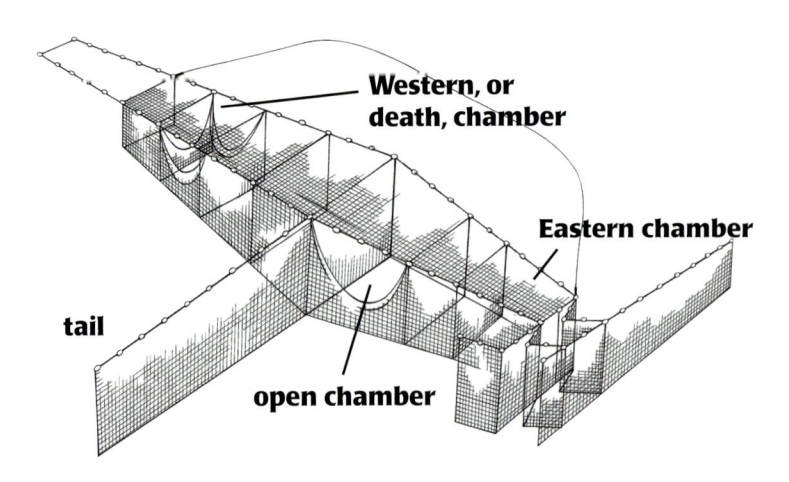

Above: For centuries, people fishing for tuna in the waters near Sicily have used a type of net called an isola (island) to catch their prey. During May and June, Sicilian fishers set out a carefully planned system of nets, lines, and buoys to guide the migrating tuna into a trap.

In the background: Fishing boats have hunted cod along the coast of Newfoundland for centuries.

Chronology

Below: A drawing of a modern tuna-fishing boat or trawler.

1972
The United States creates a law called the Marine Mammal Protection Act. One aim is to protect the accidental killing of marine mammals such as dolphins during fishing.

1992
Canada bans cod fishing in certain coastal areas because of the sharp decline in the cod population.

Bottom: The German-built *Atlantik-Supertrawler* has equipment on board to process and freeze the fish it catches in deep ocean waters.

29

Submarines

American inventor David Bushnell designed the first military submarine in 1776. Although it resembled a clam, it was called the *Turtle*. The hand-powered contraption was made of two tar-covered wooden shells, and it had room for one person. Bushnell designed the *Turtle* to be able to attach explosives to ships in a harbor. During the American Revolutionary War, a driver tried to use the contraption to attach explosives to the English ship *Eagle*, but he was unsuccessful.

Submarines are valuable in war because they are hard to find. Engineers try to design ways to make submarines travel silently through the water to make them harder to spot. In World War I, Germany used U-boats. In German the word for U-boat is *Unterseeboot* (undersea boat). The U-boats sailed on the surface much of the time, but they submerged before carrying out attacks. The Germans used the U-boats to attack ships bringing food and supplies to Europe. During World War II, the United States used its submarines to destroy many Japanese ships.

Above: A drawing shows the diving suit that European inventor Karl Heinrich Klingert created. It had a jacket and pants made of waterproof leather, a domed helmet, and a porthole connected to breathing tubes.

Right: A drawing shows a cross section of a submarine. Submarines have tanks in the space between their inner and outer hulls. The tanks are filled with air and water. To go deeper, water is added to the tanks, making the submarine heavier. To rise, water is pumped out.

Left: David Bushnell's *Turtle* design was large enough for one person.

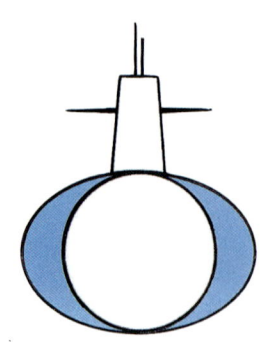

30

Chronology

1776
American inventor David Bushnell builds the *Turtle*.

1900
The U.S. Navy commissions the *Holland*, its first functional submarine.

1939
At the outbreak of World War II, the German U-30 sinks the British passenger liner *Athenia*.

Above: A German U-boat surfaces. The Germans used U-boats to attack Allied supply ships going to Europe.

Right: An Italian minisubmarine uses sonar to find and destroy mines.

In the 1950s, two new ideas made it possible for submarines to stay submerged for longer periods of time. Submarines began using nuclear power instead of fuel that had to be replaced frequently. Machines were created to extract oxygen from seawater. As a result, submarines could stay underwater for months. These changes made many new voyages possible. For example, in 1958, the USS *Nautilus* crossed the North Pole beneath the Arctic ice cap.

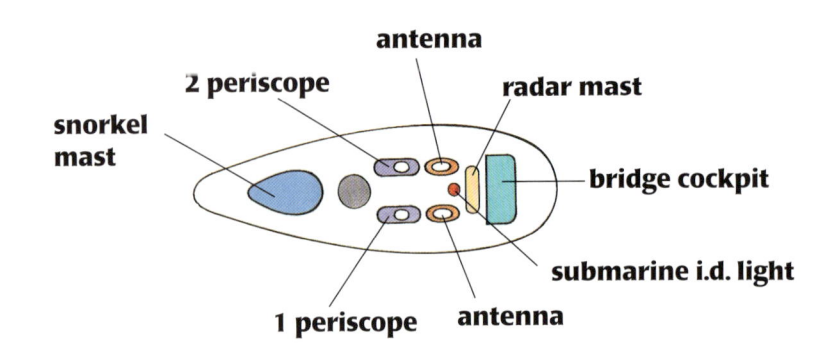

Above: A diagram shows parts of the submarine's conning tower. The conning tower is the submarine's raised observation post.

Below: A diagram shows the parts of a nuclear-powered submarine.

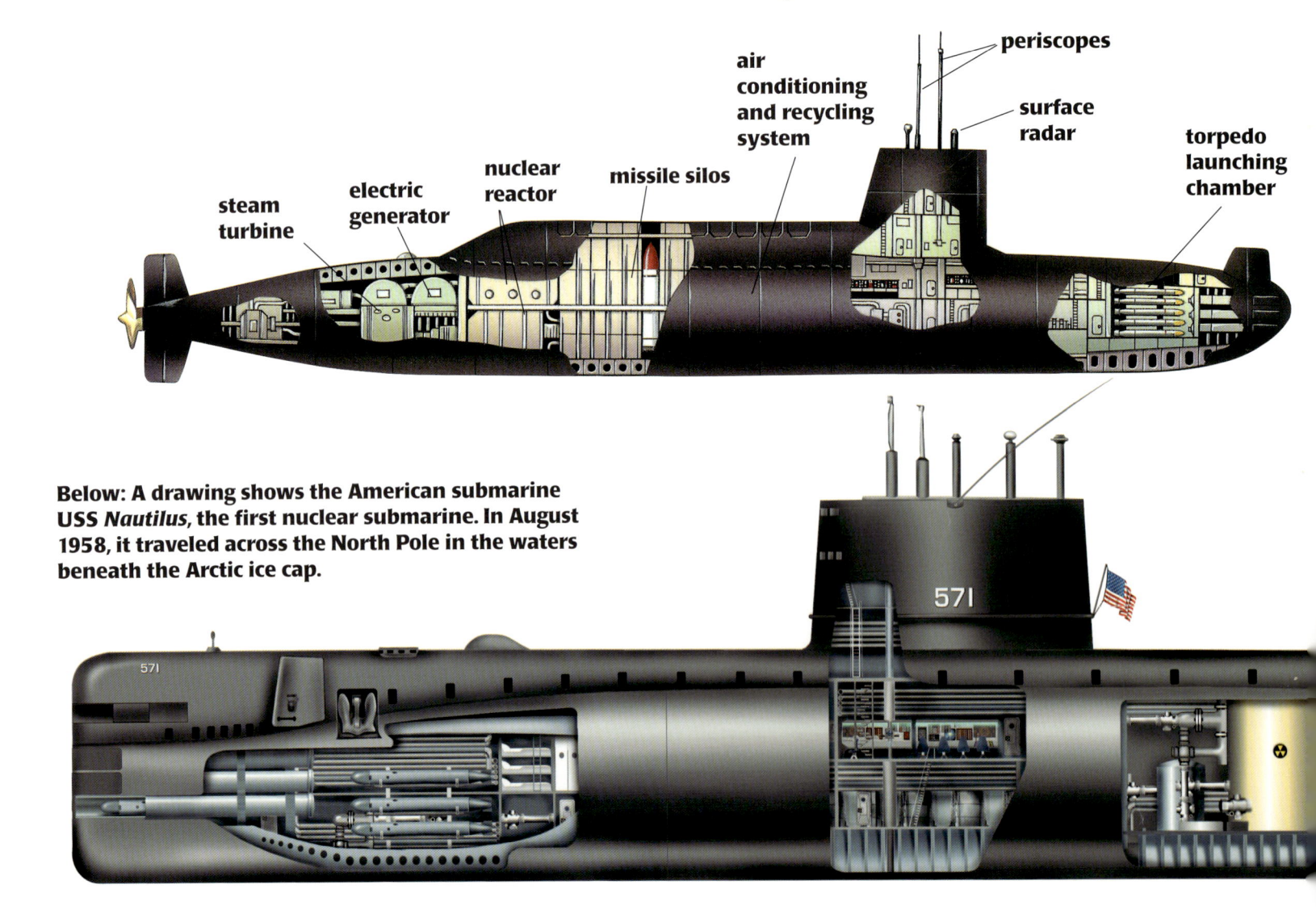

Below: A drawing shows the American submarine USS *Nautilus*, the first nuclear submarine. In August 1958, it traveled across the North Pole in the waters beneath the Arctic ice cap.

32

Chronology

1958
The U.S. Navy introduces the nuclear-powered submarine *Triton*.

1960
Jacques Picard's bathyscaphe *Trieste* ventures 35,800 feet (10,912m) to the bottom of the Challenger Deep, 200 miles (322 km) southwest of Guam. At the time this was the deepest known place on the planet.

Above: A drawing shows a diving vessel called a bathyscaphe. In 1960, Jacques Picard took a bathyscaphe named *Trieste* deeper into the ocean than anyone had ever gone before.

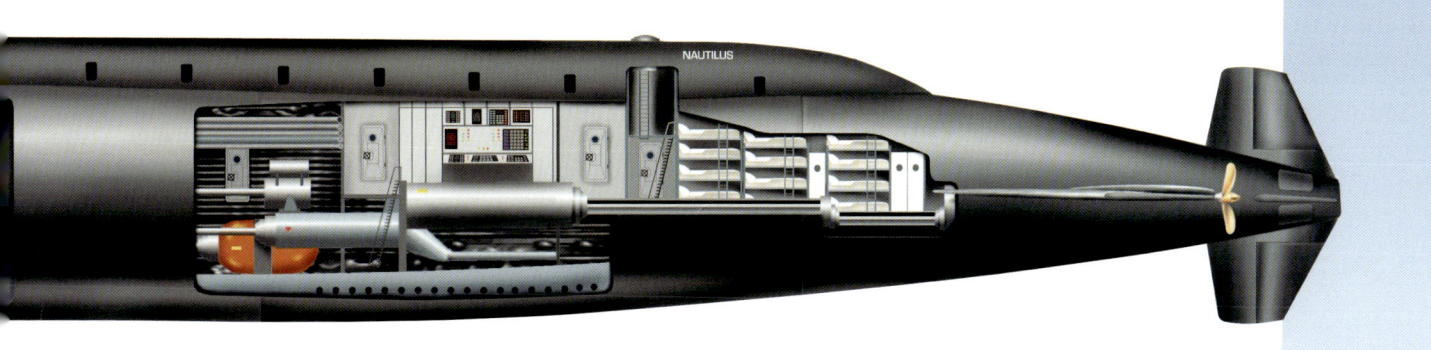

33

Unusual Ships

In the 19th century, people tried all sorts of strange-looking ship designs. Many of these odd designs did not work. One example of these unusual ships was the English *Connector*, which was built in 1863. This ship was made up of separate sections connected with huge hinges. The ship was meant to carry coal. It was expected that the *Connector* would save the crew time unloading at piers if a section of the ship could be dropped off at each destination. But the ship's design did not work. Designers knew it could not sail in rough open waters, but the *Connector* had difficulty sailing even in the calm waters of the Thames River.

Some ship designs helped people with the challenges they faced working at sea. In 1962, inventors at the University of California created a contraption called the FLIP. FLIP stands for **f**loating **i**nstrument **p**latform. As its name suggests, the craft does indeed flip. When it is traveling to its destination, a ship tows the 355-foot (108.2m) FLIP, which floats horizontally on the water. When it arrives at its destination, it flips to a vertical position. When it is vertical, its designers say it is as stable as a fencepost. The FLIP allows scientists to do research that would be impossible on a ship that moves with the motion of the sea. The U.S. Navy owns the FLIP.

Opposite, top: A drawing shows the English *Connector*. The separate sections of the ship were joined with hinges.

Below: This unusual ship design with three pairs of rollers was created by Italian Ernesto Bazin in 1896.

Below: A drawing of the *Novgorod*, a circular warship designed by Russian admiral Andrei Popov in 1873.

Chronology

Above and left: The floating instrument platform (FLIP) travels to its destination horizontally, then flips to a vertical position.

Below: The huge *Saipem 7000* is the world's largest floating crane. It has been used to lay gas pipes in the ocean.

1863
The English *Connector*, built in three hinged sections, is launched.

1873
The Russian Imperial Navy builds the circular battleship *Novgorod*.

1896
Italian Ernesto Bazin launches a ship that has three pairs of rollers attached to its hull.

1962
Inventors create the floating instrument platform (FLIP).

2002
The *Saipem 7000* finishes laying gas pipes in the Black Sea between Russia and Turkey.

Modern Warships

A navy uses many kinds of warships. Each ship has a special task, and they are used together to win wars. Naval commanders throughout the world group different ships together into teams, each with a specific task. In the U.S. Navy, for example, commanders often group ships together in what is called a "strike group." The member ships of a strike group vary, but a typical group will include five different types of ships. An aircraft carrier usually plays a central role and has support ships to travel with it. The support ships include cruisers, destroyers, submarines, and combat support ships. A cruiser is a ship with missiles that can hit faraway targets. A destroyer is a fast ship with weapons. A submarine seeks out and destroys enemy ships and other submarines. The combat support ship carries fuel, ammunition, and supplies that crews need when they are at sea for long periods of time.

Bottom left: The British aircraft carrier *Invincible* has served in wars in the Falkland Islands, Bosnia, and Iraq.

Left: A drawing shows a missile-launching device from the Italian mobile aircraft cruiser *Garibaldi*.

Right: A drawing shows a cannon on the French aircraft carrier *Clemenceau*.

Left: A drawing shows a cannon on the Russian aircraft carrier *Kiev*.

Chronology

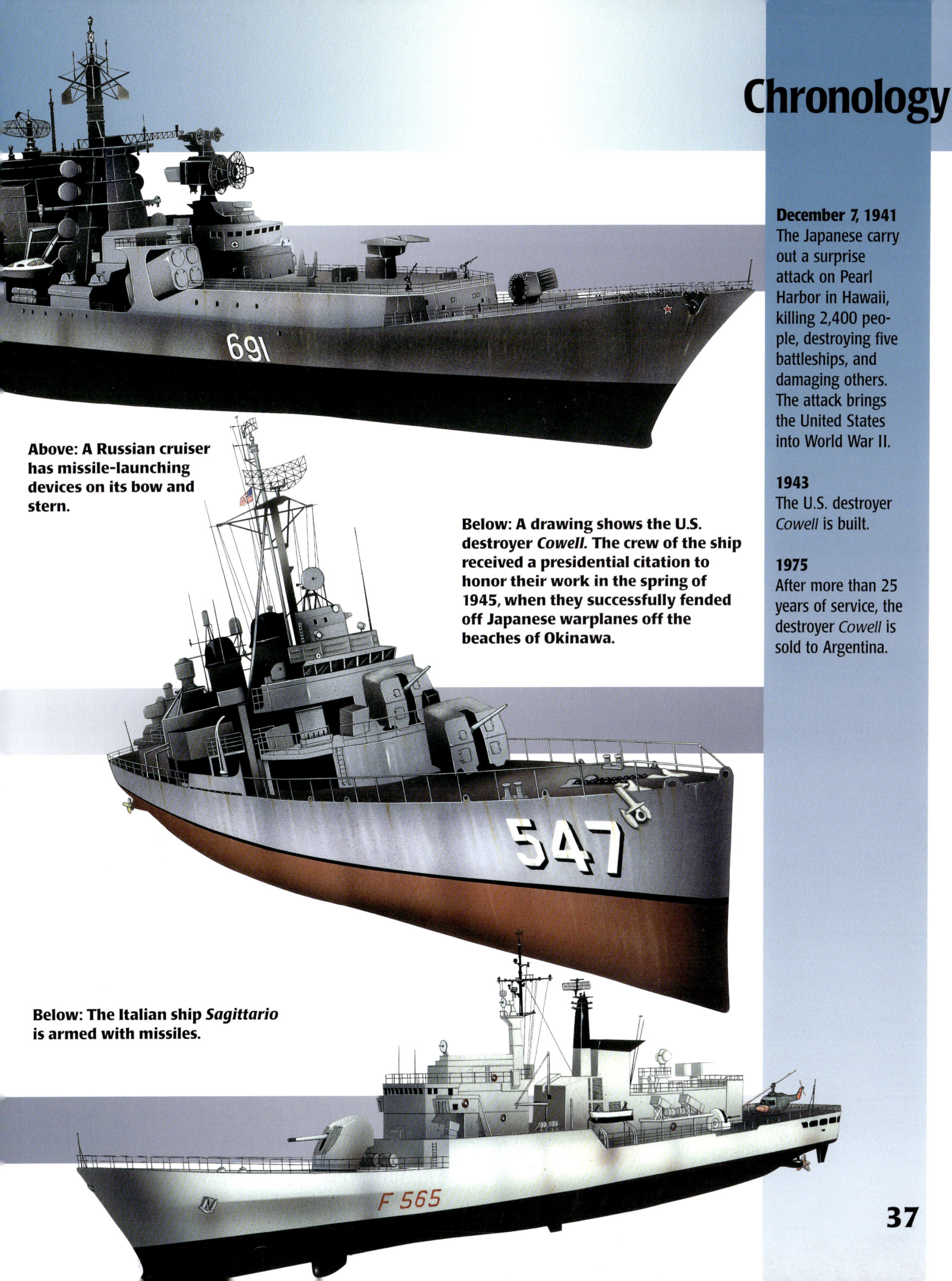

Above: A Russian cruiser has missile-launching devices on its bow and stern.

Below: A drawing shows the U.S. destroyer *Cowell*. The crew of the ship received a presidential citation to honor their work in the spring of 1945, when they successfully fended off Japanese warplanes off the beaches of Okinawa.

Below: The Italian ship *Sagittario* is armed with missiles.

December 7, 1941
The Japanese carry out a surprise attack on Pearl Harbor in Hawaii, killing 2,400 people, destroying five battleships, and damaging others. The attack brings the United States into World War II.

1943
The U.S. destroyer *Cowell* is built.

1975
After more than 25 years of service, the destroyer *Cowell* is sold to Argentina.

Supporting Warships

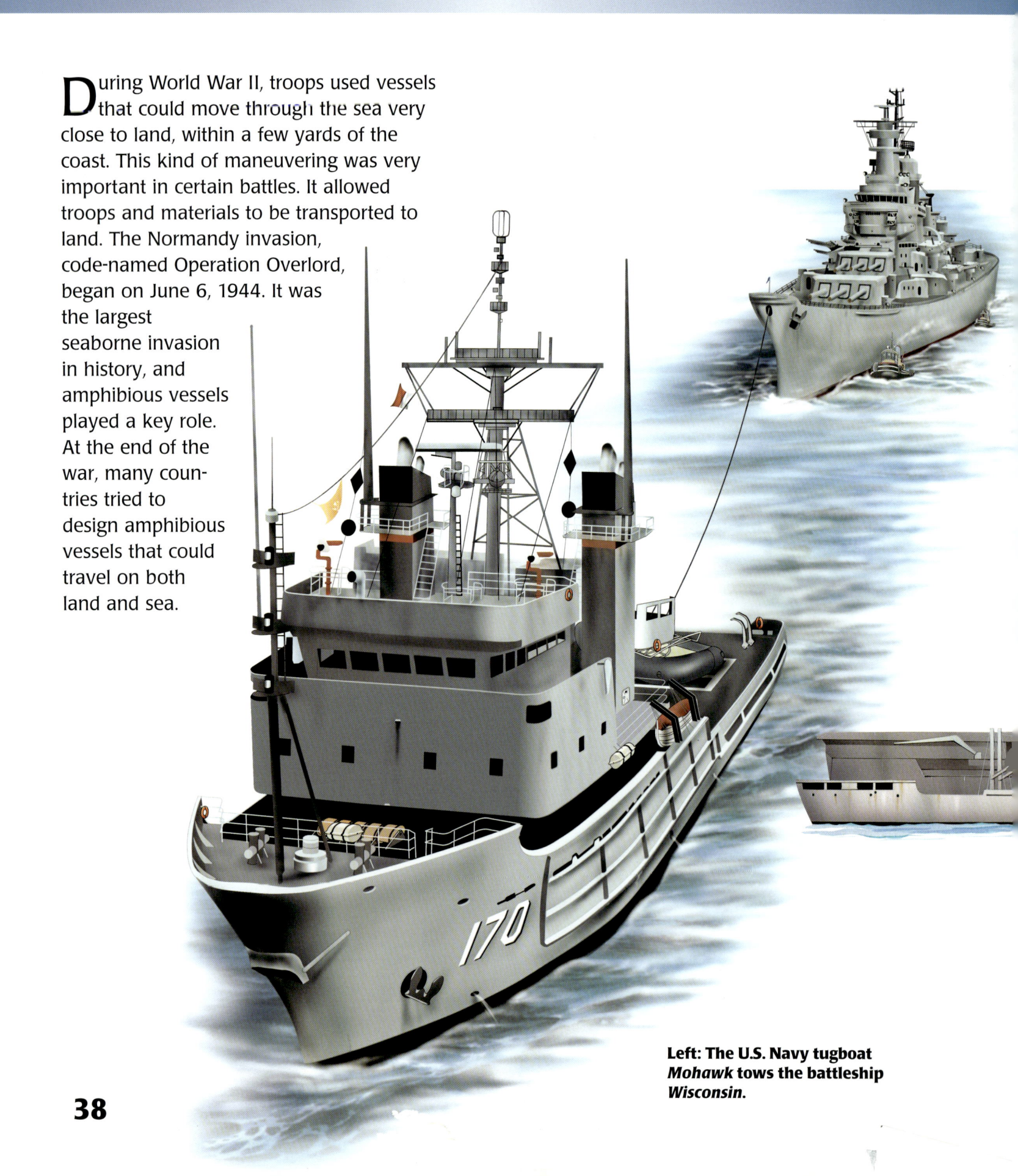

During World War II, troops used vessels that could move through the sea very close to land, within a few yards of the coast. This kind of maneuvering was very important in certain battles. It allowed troops and materials to be transported to land. The Normandy invasion, code-named Operation Overlord, began on June 6, 1944. It was the largest seaborne invasion in history, and amphibious vessels played a key role. At the end of the war, many countries tried to design amphibious vessels that could travel on both land and sea.

Left: The U.S. Navy tugboat *Mohawk* tows the battleship *Wisconsin*.

Chronology

Above: A drawing shows an amphibious armored landing vehicle. The LVTP-7 can carry up to 25 people.

Right: A photograph shows Australian troops landing in operations in Borneo during World War II.

1944
Operation Overlord brings 4,126 ships and more than 3 million troops to the beaches of Normandy in France. The invasion proves to be the turning point for the Allied forces in World War II.

1971
The LVTP-7 becomes part of the U.S. Marine Corps. It weighs 26 tons (23.6 metric tons) and can carry up to 25 marines. It can travel up to 45 miles (72km) per hour on the road and is also amphibious with water speeds up to 8 miles (14km) per hour.

Above: The support ship USS *White Plains* supplies aircraft carriers with spare parts and other supplies it may need.

Right: A landing craft is capable of taking people and vehicles to shore.

Aircraft Carriers

The aircraft carrier is the largest ship in a modern navy. It is also one of the most important military ships. Aircraft carriers are floating airfields. They allow military aircraft to land and take off in far-off regions of the world, without having to depend on land bases.

The first aircraft carriers were tested in the early part of the 20th century. An American pilot named Eugene Ely became the first person to take off from a ship in 1910. The following year, he landed on the USS *Pennsylvania* as it was anchored in San Francisco Bay. Ten countries have aircraft carriers: Brazil, China, France, India, Italy, Russia, Spain, Thailand, the United Kingdom, and the United States.

Right: The nuclear-powered aircraft carrier USS *Enterprise* is the world's fastest aircraft carrier. The *Enterprise* cruises at more than 30 knots, which is more than 35 miles (56 km) per hour. A crew of 5,500 sailors runs the ship.

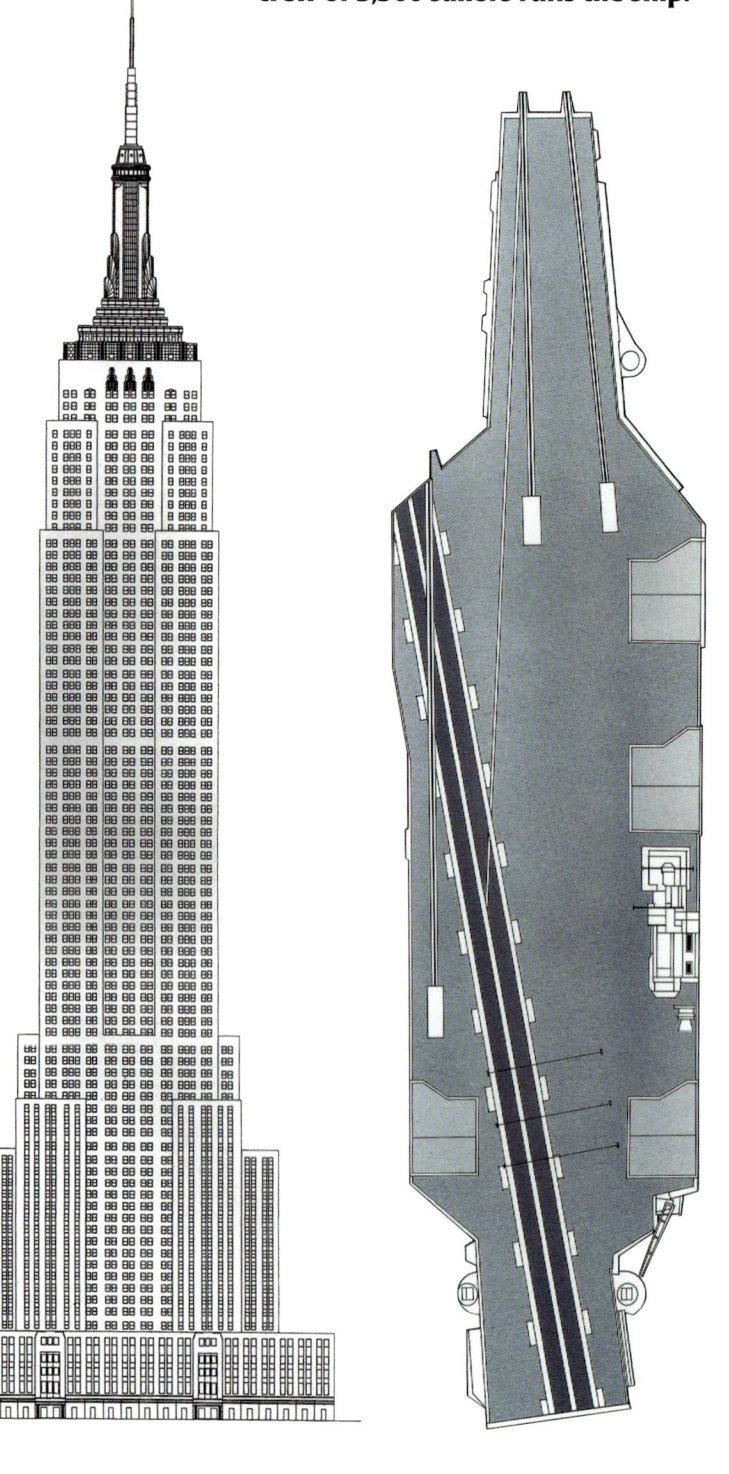

Right: If the USS *Enterprise* were set vertically on its stern, it would be almost as tall as the Empire State Building in New York City.

40

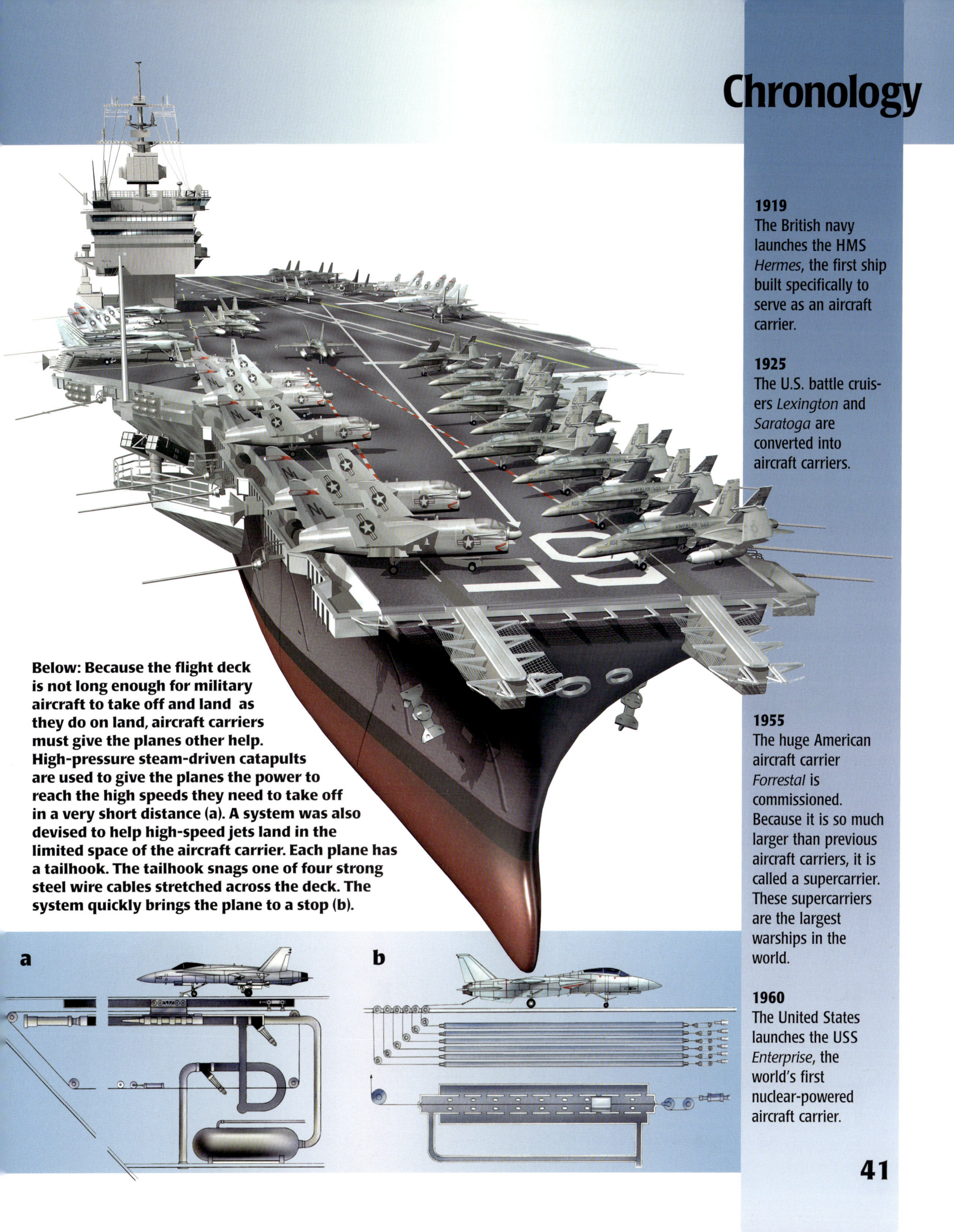

Chronology

1919
The British navy launches the HMS *Hermes*, the first ship built specifically to serve as an aircraft carrier.

1925
The U.S. battle cruisers *Lexington* and *Saratoga* are converted into aircraft carriers.

1955
The huge American aircraft carrier *Forrestal* is commissioned. Because it is so much larger than previous aircraft carriers, it is called a supercarrier. These supercarriers are the largest warships in the world.

1960
The United States launches the USS *Enterprise*, the world's first nuclear-powered aircraft carrier.

Below: Because the flight deck is not long enough for military aircraft to take off and land as they do on land, aircraft carriers must give the planes other help. High-pressure steam-driven catapults are used to give the planes the power to reach the high speeds they need to take off in a very short distance (a). A system was also devised to help high-speed jets land in the limited space of the aircraft carrier. Each plane has a tailhook. The tailhook snags one of four strong steel wire cables stretched across the deck. The system quickly brings the plane to a stop (b).

41

Signals at Sea

For centuries, people at sea have found ways to communicate with one another, even when they do not speak the same language. Over the years, sailors have devised a language of the sea that uses flags. Using a certain arrangement of flags, sailors can send messages to people on other ships quickly. For example, one combination of flags means, "Stop your vessel instantly." Another combination means, "You are risking running aground." People at sea sometimes use a pair of handheld flags to spell out messages letter by letter. This code is called the semaphore flag signaling system.

Right: An 18th-century drawing shows a cross section of a lighthouse. This lighthouse uses both lights and fog bells to help guide ships. Lighthouses help ships find the entrance to harbors and avoid areas of danger.

Below: The flag positions form each letter of the alphabet in the semaphore flag signaling system.

42

Chronology

Oscar **Lima** **Juliet** **Victor**

Left: Drawings show some of the alphabet flags that are used for international signals at sea. Each flag represents a specific letter, which is the first letter of the flag's name.

November **Charlie** **Uniform** **Wischey**

Below: Ships send important messages quickly when the flags are arranged in pairs, one on top of another, according to a code. Drawings show the messages from four pairs of flags.

1835
U.S. inventor Samuel F.B. Morse builds his first telegraph.

1844
The first Morse code message is transmitted.

stop your vessel instantly

I am abandoning ship

keep well clear of me

you are running the risk of going aground

0 1 2 3 4
5 6 7 8 9

Above: Pennants represent numbers.

Below: At night, sailors use lights on ships and boats to communicate their positions and actions. Ships display a combination of red, green, and white lights in a pattern to give other ships a message. The drawings show lights on top of a sailboat mast (a), on a fishing boat (b), and on a ship that is grounded (c).

Right: A chart shows the Morse code alphabet. Developed by Samuel Morse in 1835, the code allows people to communicate, letter by letter. The code uses short and long signals, represented here by dots (for short signals) and dashes (for long signals).

A	.—	N	—.
B	—...	O	———
C	—.—.	P	.——.
D	—..	Q	——.—
E	.	R	.—.
F	..—.	S	...
G	——.	T	—
H	....	U	..—
I	..	V	...—
J	.———	W	.——
K	—.—	X	—..—
L	.—..	Y	—.——
M	——	Z	——..

a b 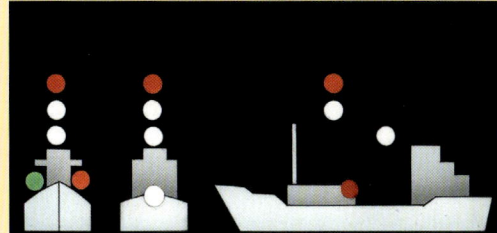 c

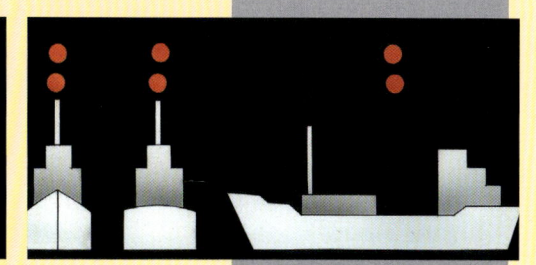

Pleasure Boats

Though boats and ships are used for work and for war, many are built and used simply for pleasure. Recreational boats may be built of wood or metal. Many modern recreational boats are built of man-made materials such as fiberglass. These man-made materials can be molded into just the shape boatmakers want. They are also easier to take care of than wood or metal. Most speedboats made for pleasure have hulls that are flat at the stern (rear) of the boat. That makes the boat slide through the water more easily. The front of the boat is usually V-shaped to make the boat stable.

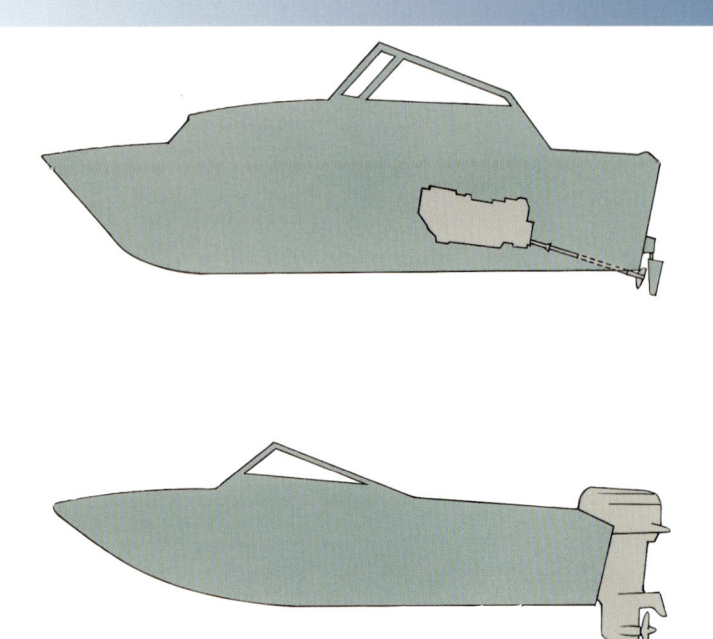

Top left: A drawing shows a toy motorboat made of tin.

Above: Motors are attached to pleasure boats in several ways. The top drawing shows a boat with an inboard motor. As the name suggests, inboard motors are built into the ship. The bottom drawing shows an outboard motor. Outboard motors can be removed from the boat.

Below: A drawing shows the *Rain-X Challenger*. Craig Arfons designed the craft to be the fastest boat in the world, but when he tried to set the world record, the boat crashed, and he was killed.

Below: A drawing shows a high-speed powerboat. These boats are used in racing competitions. Australian Ken Warby holds the world water speed record. In 1978, he set the record, going 317.6 miles (511.1 km) per hour.

44

Chronology

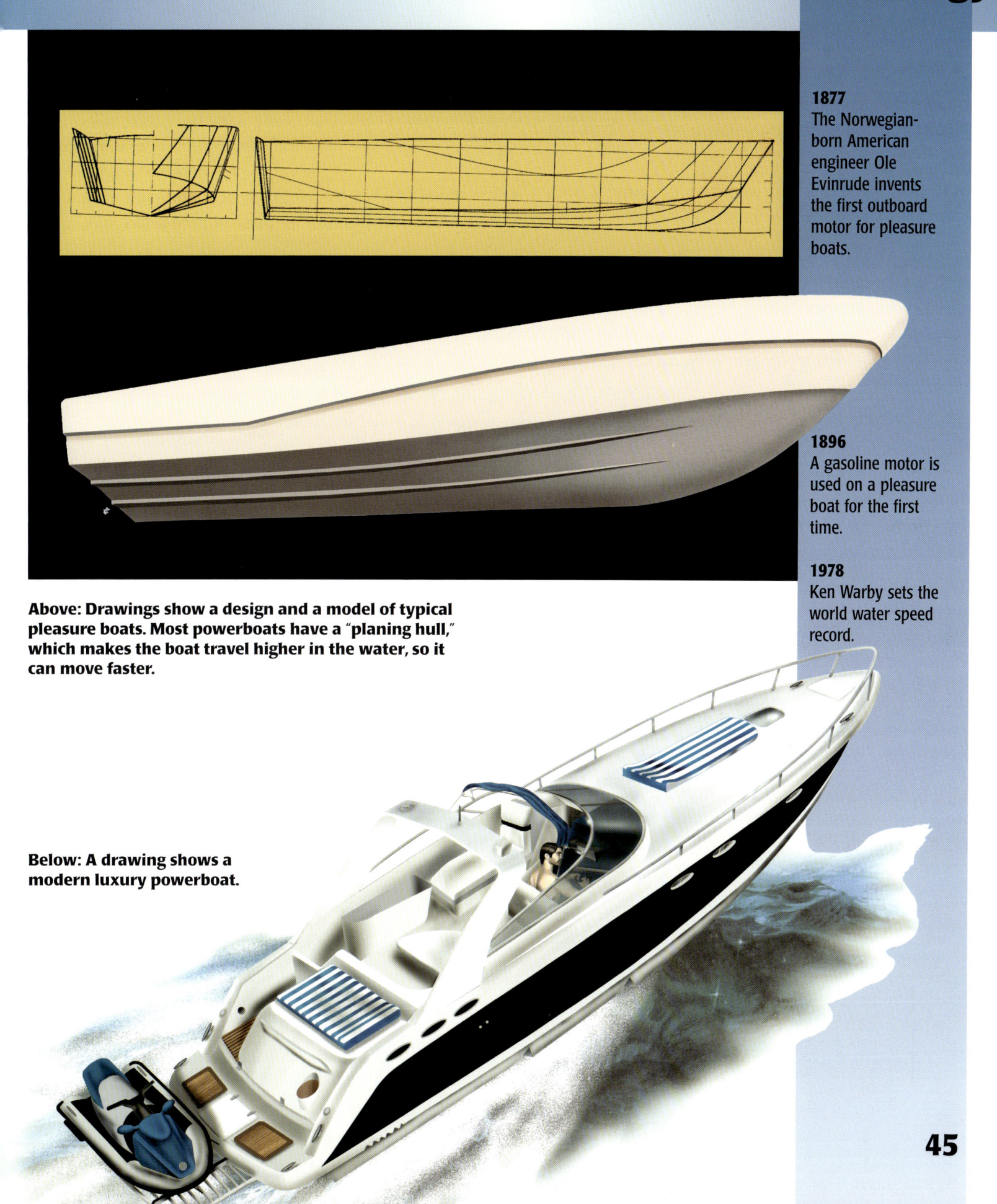

1877
The Norwegian-born American engineer Ole Evinrude invents the first outboard motor for pleasure boats.

1896
A gasoline motor is used on a pleasure boat for the first time.

1978
Ken Warby sets the world water speed record.

Above: Drawings show a design and a model of typical pleasure boats. Most powerboats have a "planing hull," which makes the boat travel higher in the water, so it can move faster.

Below: A drawing shows a modern luxury powerboat.

45

Glossary

amphibious: Able to operate on both land and water.

bathyscaphe: An underwater vessel that can reach the deepest waters of the ocean.

Civil War: A war fought from 1861 until 1865 in the United States between the Northern and Southern states.

conning tower: The raised observation post of a submarine.

cruiser: A warship that is faster and smaller than a battleship.

dock: A place where a ship's cargo and passengers are loaded and unloaded.

dry dock: A place where ships can be taken out of the water for repairs and maintenance.

freighters: Ships used chiefly to carry freight.

horizontal: Parallel to the horizon.

hull: The frame or body of a boat or ship.

hydrofoil: A boat that is designed to lift out of the water as it moves at high speeds.

junk: A flat-bottomed Chinese sailing ship.

knot: The measure of speed of a ship, about 1.15 miles (2.13 km) per hour.

Morse code: A system used to send messages by radio or with flashes of light. Each letter is represented by one or more short signals, called dots, and long signals, called dashes.

paddle wheel: A wheel with boards or paddles around its rim that propels a ship.

powerboat: A motorboat that is usually designed for racing.

propeller: A device with blades mounted on a hub. As the propeller turns, it moves air or water, which makes the force to drive a boat or plane forward.

sonar: (**so**und **n**avigation **a**nd **r**anging) A device that uses sound waves to locate objects in the water.

steerage: The part of the ship for passengers paying the lowest fare. Steerage is on one of the ship's lower decks, and the name comes from the steering devices that once were located on these bottom decks.

stern: The back of a boat or ship.

tatami: Straw mats used in Japan.

trawling: Fishing with a large net that is dragged along the bottom of the ocean.

tugboat: A small, powerful boat used for guiding large ships into port.

U-boat: A type of submarine used by the Germans in World War II. The U stood for *Unterseeboot* (undersea boat).

vertical: Perpendicular to the horizon.

World War I: A world conflict that took place from 1914 to 1918.

World War II: A world conflict that began in 1939 and ended in 1945.

For More Information

Carol Baldwin, *U.S. Navy Fighting Vessels.* Chicago: Heinemann, 2004.

Mark Dartford, *Warships.* Minneapolis, MN: Lerner, 2004.

Ole Steen Hansen, *Seaplanes and Naval Aviation.* New York: Crabtree, 2004.

Paul Kupperberg, *The Tragedy of the Titanic.* New York: Rosen, 2003.

Phillip Margulies, *The Exxon Valdez Oil Spill.* New York: Rosen, 2003.

Bradford Matsen, *The Incredible Quest to Find the Titanic.* Berkeley Heights, NJ: Enslow, 2003.

Arlene Bourgeois Molzahn, *Ships and Boats.* Berkeley Heights, NJ: Enslow, 2003.

Walter Dean Myers, *USS Constellation: Pride of the American Navy.* New York: Holiday House, 2004.

Elaine Pascoe, ed. *Seawolf Submarine.* San Diego, CA: Blackbirch, 2004.

Morris A. Pierce, *Robert Fulton and the Development of the Steamboat.* New York: PowerKids Press, 2003.

Pam Rosenberg, *Robert Fulton: Engineer and Inventor.* Chanhassen, MN: Child's World, 2003.

Greg Roza, *The Incredible Story of Aircraft Carriers.* New York: Rosen, 2004.

Brian Wingate, *Submariners: Life in Submarines.* New York: Rosen, 2004.

Index

Aaron Manby, 11
aircraft carrier, 36, 39, 40–41
Alecto, 11
Amoco-Cadiz, 27
amphibious vessels, 38, 39
Aquitania, 19
Arfons, Craig, 44
Arpad, 7
Atlantik-Supertrawler, 29

bathyscaphe, 33
battleships, 12–13, 38
Bazin, Ernesto, 34, 35
Bell, Alexander Graham, 21
Bismarck, 13
Braman, Joseph, 7
British Admiral, 27
Brunel, Isambard Kingdom, 10
Bushnell, David, 30, 31

cargo, 22, 26
Charlotte Dundas, 7
Clemenceau, 36
Clermont, 8
coal, 8, 10, 34
Cockerell, Christopher, 20
cod, 28, 29
combat support ships, 36
communication, 19, 42–43
Connector, 34–35
Cowell, 37
crane, 22, 23, 35
cruisers, 36, 37

deep-sea fishing, 28–29
de Lôme, Dupuy, 13
destroyers, 36
Devastation, 13
dolphins, 28, 29
double hulled ships, 26–27
dry dock, 22

Eagle, 30
Elettra, 19
Ely, Eugene, 40
Enterprise, 40, 41
Evinrude, Ole, 45

Exxon Valdez, 26

factory ships, 24, 29
ferryboats, 20–21
fishing, commercial, 24, 25, 28–29
flags, 42–43
FLIP (floating instrument platform), 34, 35
Forlanini, Enrico, 21
Forrestal, 41
Fulton, Robert, 8, 9

Garibaldi, 36
Glomar Challenger, 24, 25
Glückauf, 26
Great Britain, 10, 11
Great Eastern, 10, 11
Great Western, 8

Harrisburg, 23
Hermes, 41
hovercrafts, 20–21
hull, 10, 12, 13, 14, 17, 20, 26, 30, 44, 45
Hulls, Jonathan, 7
hydrofoils, 20–21

icebreakers, 24, 25
immigrants, 18
Invincible, 36
iron, 12
iron giants, 10–11

Jahre Viking, 26
jets, 41

Kamo Maru, 19
Kiev, 36
Klingert, Karl Heinrich, 30

La Gloire, 12, 13
landing craft, 39
Leonardo da Vinci, 6
Lexington, 41
lighthouse, 42
lights, 42, 43
longshoremen, 22
luxury liners, 14–15, 16, 19

LVTP-7, 39

Marconi, Guglielmo, 19
Marine Mammal Protection Act, 29
Mauretania, 15, 19
Merrimack, 12
missiles, 36, 37
Mohawk, 38
Monitor, 12
Morse code, 43
motors, 44, 45

Nautilus, 32–33
nets, fishing, 28
Nimitz, 40
Normandie, 15
Normandy invasion, 38, 39
North River Steamboat, 8
Novgorod, 34, 35
nuclear power, 32, 33, 40, 41

ocean liners, 14–15, 16, 18
oil-drilling ships, 24, 25, 26
oil spills, 26–27
Operation Overlord, 38, 39

paddleboat, 8
paddle wheels, 6, 7, 10, 11
Papin, Denis, 7
Pelican, 24
Pennsylvania, 40
Phoenix, 9
Picard, Jacques, 33
planing hull, 45
pleasure boats, 44–45
Popov, Andrei, 34
ports, 22–23
powerboats, 44, 45
Prestige, 27
propellers, 7, 10, 11

Queen Elizabeth, 15, 19
Queen Mary, 15, 19

radio, 19
Radisson Diamond, 14
Rain-X Challenger, 44

Rattler, 11
recreational boats, 44–45
Rex, 15

Sagittario, 37
sails, 8, 9, 13
Saipem 7000, 35
Saratoga, 41
Savannah, 8, 9
signals, 42–43
Sirius, 8, 9
Small-Waterplane-Area Twin-Hull (SWATH) ship, 14
sonar, 28, 31
speedboats, 44
SRN-7, 21
steamboat, 7
steam engine, 7, 9, 11
steamship, 6, 7, 8–9, 10, 11, 16, 18
steerage, 18–19
strike group, 36
submarines, 30–33, 36

tankers, 26–27
Tina Onassis, 27
Titanic, 16–17
trawler, 29
Trieste, 33
Triton, 33
tugboat, 7, 23, 38
tuna, 28, 29
Turtle, 30, 31

U-boats, 30

Virginia, 12

Warby, Ken, 44, 45
Warrior, 12, 13
warships, 12, 13, 34, 36–37, 38–39
weapons, 36
White Plains, 39
William Rockefeller, 27
Wisconsin, 38
World War I, 13, 19, 30
World War II, 13, 15, 30, 37, 38, 39

48